SKILLS

ACTION

SAGE COUNSELLING *IN ACTION*

Series Editor: WINDY DRYDEN

Sage Counselling in Action is a series of short, practical books developed especially for students and trainees. As accessible introductions to theory and practice, they have become core texts for many courses, both in counselling and other professions such as nursing, social work, teaching and management. Books in the series include:

INTEGRATIVE
COUNSELLING SKILLS
IN ACTION

Second Edition

Sue Culley *and*
Tim Bond

SAGE Publications
London ● Thousand Oaks ● New Delhi

ISBN 0-7619-6993-4 (hbk)
ISBN 0-7619-6994-2 (pbk)
© Sue Culley and Tim Bond 1991, 2004
First published 1991
Reprinted three times
Second edition 2004
Reprinted 2005, 2006

SAGE Publications Ltd
1 Oliver's Yard
55 City Road
London EC1Y 1SP

SAGE Publications Inc
2455 Teller Road
Thousand Oaks
California 91320

SAGE Publications India Pvt. Ltd
B–42 Panchsheel Enclave
PO Box 4109
New Delhi 110 017

British Library Cataloguing in Publication data
A catalogue record for this book is available from the British Library

Library of Congress Control Number: 2003115421

Printed on paper from sustainable sources

Typeset by M Rules, Southwark, London
Printed and bound in Great Britain by
Cromwell Press Limited, Trowbridge, Wiltshire

Contents

1

LEARNING COUNSELLING SKILLS

Counselling skills have been one of the most exciting and influential developments in a wide variety of helping relationships. We have learned from the feedback to the first edition written by Sue Culley (Culley, 1991: 30) that this book has been used far more widely than in professional counselling training. A wide range of caring professions including medicine and nursing, social work, human resource management, and pastoral care in schools and religious communities has successfully applied the insights associated with counselling skills. These skills are also widely used in the rapidly developing fields of life coaching and mentoring. Although most of the known applications of counselling skills tend to be professional relationships, they are also used in voluntary and less formal settings. We have heard of counselling skills being used to help to train people, often young people, in a variety of peer support schemes. One of the reasons why the co-author of the second edition, Tim Bond, was keen to be involved in writing this book is his experience of training people in the use of counselling skills in healthcare, education and community groups. This new edition has been written to take account of the wide range of potential applications for using counselling skills.

However, neither of us has wanted to lose sight of the significance of counselling skills to professional counselling training. Skills training is a required component of most training in counselling, psychotherapy and applied psychology. As the name indicates, 'counselling skills' have their origins in the evolution of counselling. They were developed in response to a quest for what distinguished the effective from the less effective practitioner. It was realised that, in order to be competent, counsellors required more than emotional insight and a relevant pool of knowledge; they also needed to be able to communicate effectively. Feelings, insight and knowledge have little impact unless they can be articulated. This realisation has expanded the focus of attention beyond the *content* of the communication to the *process*; it is not simply what you communicate but how you communicate. One of the pioneering studies that informed the development of counselling skills analysed and described the microskills used by counsellors in the United States (Truax and Carkhuff, 1967: 18). Many other studies have built on this work by developing strategies and recommended combinations of skills to assist with both problem-solving and enhancing social competence. One of the characteristics of these later developments in counselling skills is that, while they frequently had their origins in attempts to address issues that arose in counselling, they have also since been recognised as applying more widely to a variety of helping relationships (Aldridge et al., 2001; Freshwater, 2003; King, 1999; Tschudin, 1995; Ross, 2003). We are continuing in this tradition.

When we reflected on our own experience of counselling skills, we realised that we draw heavily upon them in a wide variety of different types of roles and relationships. Sue works extensively in the corporate sector, delivering skills training for both line and human resources managers; she also coaches and mediates as well as supports those who have been subjected to harassment and bullying. Tim is Director of a large international postgraduate programme and uses counselling skills in both academic and personal tutorials as well as in his research and consultancy concerning professional ethics. With this wide range of applications, we have needed to find words that identify the users of counselling skills and the person being helped. There are no totally satisfactory role-labels but we have decided to follow the latest practice in the British Association for Counselling and Psychotherapy. We are using the term 'practitioner' for the user of counselling skills and hope that the reader will substitute a more role-appropriate label, if this required. For the same reasons, we are using the term 'client' for the recipient of counselling skills. Again, some readers may wish to substitute a term that is more appropriate to the context in which they practise.

Counselling, along with many other types of helping relationships, shares a number of challenges that can be greatly helped by the use of counselling skills. This book is structured around a straightforward theoretical framework that provides a 'template' for guiding and shaping the process from initiation to closure by:

1   *Establishing an appropriate relationship.* The fundamental foundations of counselling skills direct our attention to how we develop, sustain and evaluate relationships; to the impact of non-verbal communication and to the interpersonal skills typically used in everyday problem-solving.

2   *Constructing a way of working together that is focused on addressing specific problems or issues.* The beginning or foundation skills mark out this way of helping as being essentially different from everyday conversation. The skills provide the means for establishing a shared understanding about the purpose of talking together, of exploring and gathering information in ways that facilitate mutual understanding of the concerns of the person wanting help.

3   *Discovering new ways of seeing the problem or issue to empower the person affected.* Simply sharing the problem may not be sufficient in itself. Some may need the further help of a variety of considered challenges and inputs that open up new and better possibilities for them.

4   *Supporting the implementation of any actions required to resolve the issue presented.* The gap between talking in a supportive relationship and putting a plan into action in what may be less supportive circumstances can seem daunting. Counselling skills offer strategies for helping someone to make the transition from words to action.

5   *Challenging situations that can arise when using counselling skills.* One of the sources of perpetual interest in using counselling skills is that every person and issue is different. A successful practitioner typically has a high tolerance of uncertainty as the helping process unfolds, together with a readiness to respond to the unexpected. Some preparation for responding to surprising and challenging situations helps to develop confidence. Preparation also enhances the practitioner's capacity to keep potentially overwhelming situations contained and safe for both the person being helped and themselves.

In our experience, the idea of stages is beneficial to learning and applying counselling skills. Stages provide a kind of navigation aid for the practitioner in identifying what strategies and skills might be relevant. The actual practice of counselling is invariably not so well ordered. The person seeking help is neither required to read about counselling skills nor to have trained in them. They are not required to fit the textbook. They may present their story in any way they like, even if this changes or complicates the sequence of the stages. Nevertheless, to be able to respond to the potential complexity of using counselling skills, it is best to become familiar with the stages as they are presented in Chapters 4–6.

Distinguishing Counselling from Other Ways of Helping

The wide range of potential applications of counselling skills to different ways of helping makes them a valuable asset and well worth learning. The range of applications is endless. You can use them to support a friend with problems, help a colleague decide whether to stop smoking, respond to an indecisive customer, clarify what is concerning someone who wants to make a complaint, and for a multitude of other purposes. They can be used in an enormous variety of settings, ranging from informal ones like the home and social groups to more formally structured contexts like voluntary, commercial or statutory organisations. A good grasp of counselling skills is an enormous asset in human resource management and any type of caring role.

However, all assets can also become problematic and counselling skills are no exception. The many different applications of these skills may become a source of potential confusion that frustrates the user and confuses the recipient of whatever type of service is being offered.

Consider the following example. A teacher is in the process of disciplining a pupil for not doing any homework. The pupil reveals for the first time that her parents have just separated and she has to look after younger brothers and sisters so that her mother can go to work. The teacher is genuinely shocked not to have known this and changes her approach from reprimanding to using counselling skills to learn about the new circumstances and to help the pupil consider the choices open to her. The teacher is an experienced welfare tutor and adept in counselling skills. The pupil desperately wants to find a source of support and understanding. The switch from being 'told off' to caring about her well-being confuses her and leaves her feeling vulnerable. She feels a strong urge to tell everything but how far should she go? If she starts to say how much she misses her dad, will she be able to stop herself from saying how she mistrusts her mother's new boyfriend who has made sexual advances to her and how she worries when her younger brothers and sisters are left unsupervised? Will the teacher help her to think things through or insist on bringing in the authorities? This is the sort of situation most teachers and many pupils will recognise. The confusing start to the conversation and switch in purpose from punishment to care makes it much more difficult to achieve a positive outcome. If the pupil remains sullenly silent, not only has she lost the opportunity for help but may provoke a renewal of the original recriminations over missing homework. If she responds to the empathy and 'tells all', will she later regret it and feel betrayed by what she may have experienced as manipulative techniques? Throughout, the teacher is well-intentioned towards the pupil but the lack of clarity over her role, purpose and intent may create the very mistrust that she is striving to avoid. Similar confusions can arise in healthcare unless the boundaries between a clinician offering expert opinion and facilitating a patient in making a decision about future healthcare are clearly signalled. The effective use of counselling skills requires the practitioner to be clear about the purpose of the conversation with the person being helped in order to avoid misunderstandings that might inhibit the client or lead to inappropriate expectations.

Another potential source of confusion exists in the distinction between formal counselling and using counselling skills. This distinction can be extremely significant in some contexts. For example, counselling skills can be used to advantage by almost anyone to offer support to a colleague in the workplace. In this context, one of the potential sources of confusion is whether the help is being offered to further the organisation's aims or those of the person receiving help. Good practice in counselling skills demands clarity about whose aims are being served. However, this alone does not transform using counselling skills into counselling.

Formal counselling is increasingly recognised as a professional role with its own distinctive requirements, practices and systems of accountability. Table 1 summarises some of the key features that distinguish offering supportive help enhanced by counselling skills from formal counselling. Reputable counselling will be provided under the auspices of a professional body, such as the British Association for Counselling and Psychotherapy, governed by ethical guidelines and supported by non-managerial super-vision. Training in counselling skills is often a first step towards becoming a counsellor; but should not be confused with the extensive and profession-ally validated training that is stipulated for counsellors.

The Rewards of Learning Counselling Skills

Learning counselling skills can be an immensely rewarding and enjoyable experience. Enduring friendships have developed between course partic-ipants as they share their own life experiences in skills practice sessions. We have both had experience of highly knowledgeable professionals who have found renewed personal commitment and satisfaction in their work as they have developed better ways of communicating and relating.

Table 1   *Distinction between counselling and using counselling skills*

	Counselling	Supportive help using counselling skills
Role	Explicitly identified as a counsellor to clients; strives to avoid or minimise any role conflict and ambiguity.	Combines offering support with other roles; may involve some role conflict and role ambiguity.
Authority	Has neither managerial nor other formal authority over client.	May have managerial or other formal authority over client.
Contract	Explicit agreement to offer counselling to client including clarity about confidentiality and boundaries.	Uses discretion about whether to have a contract or to use counselling skills spontaneously. Confidentiality often implicit and boundaries may not be explicitly defined.
Time	Planned and protected from interruptions.	May not be planned; can be a spontaneous response to someone needing help.
Professional support	Works to ethical guidelines that require regular supervision to enhance quality of service.	May not have either a professional ethical framework or receive supervision.
Process	Assists clients to make their *own* decisions and take action for themselves.	May advise, coach, distribute physical resources or act on behalf of clients.
Focus	The 'person in context': the client is at the centre; the context provides a perspective for both self and practitioner assessment. The goals and aims of others are considered to the extent that they relate to the client.	The 'person and context(s)': the helper may have a dual focus and be required to take account of the context in which the help is offered. For example, to balance organisational needs and requirements with those of the individual seeking help.

Perhaps the most rewarding aspect of learning counselling skills is the way it opens up the possibility of reaching beyond the limits of one's own life to hearing how other others experience their lives. Hearing how differently people approach the inevitable challenges of relationships, work and leisure and discovering where they find a sense of meaning and purpose is an immense privilege. It can be a life-changing experience, inspiring and, at times, deeply moving. It can also be humbling to be working with someone who is coping with situations better than we might do, if the positions were to be reversed. Many years of working in our respective ranges of roles have taught us both an appreciation of the struggle that life entails for most people. It has also fostered a deep respect for the resilience, courage and resourcefulness of our clients. Using counselling skills can be a life-enhancing activity. It can result in you receiving at least as much as you give, although this may not be the reason why you started.

This book will primarily be concerned with understanding the purpose of various counselling skills and how to acquire and use the relevant techniques. This focus on techniques is inevitable in a book on this topic. However, we don't want to lose sight of the presence and influence of the person using these techniques. Intentionally or otherwise, you will be using your own life experience to inform your decisions about choosing one strategy over another.

Essential to learning counselling skills and integrating them into your personal counselling style is the process of self-evaluation and personal review. It is frequently a powerful and absorbing learning experience. Therefore we want to open this book by looking behind the techniques and by inviting you to consider what you are bringing to your work with your clients, the ethics of undertaking this role, and to prepare you for the learning process.

Using Your Personal Resourcefulness and Experience

Helping another person effectively is a surprisingly complex matter. We can easily become so absorbed in the challenge of trying to understand what is being communicated that we lose sight of how the client experiences the process. They may not be aware of the skills that you are using. They may look behind the techniques and focus their attention on their sense of *you* as a person, gauging whether you can be trusted with their intimate thoughts and whether you will be able to help them. One way into self-understanding is to reflect on our own life story. Knowing how you have responded to the challenges in your life will help you to understand why you prefer some strategies and skills to others. It will help you to identify your strengths and resourcefulness that you can bring to your use of counselling skills.

We have produced a list of questions that you may wish to return to from time to time for personal reflection or discussion:

What has helped you?

- What challenges have you faced in your life?
- How far have you resolved these challenges?
- What sorts of interventions from other people have helped or hindered?
- What did you do that helped or hindered?
- What have you learned from these experiences that will inform how you help other people?
- What strengths and resources will you bring to your use of counselling skills?
- What are the skills you want to develop further?

You may want to keep a note of your responses to these questions. Some of your answers may change as you learn counselling skills. Being aware of these changes will extend your self-awareness.

Being Ethical

Counselling skills can be extremely powerful and using them can elicit information from people that might not otherwise have been disclosed. Using these skills also places the practitioner in a very powerful and influential position. They are, of course, skills that can be applied for many purposes. For example, some of the techniques are also used in investigations, disciplinary hearings and cross-examination. Some of the strategies and skills are also used in direct selling and marketing; most notably in the rapport-building phase and bringing the sale to a conclusion. The diversity of ways and of the contexts in which they can be deployed emphasises the significance of ethical awareness in their use. For example, would it be ethical for a human resources manager to use these skills in order to acquire sensitive and confidential information from an employee for the purpose of building a case to retire that employee early, against the employee's known wishes? Would the use of counselling skills in order to influence the employee into accepting early retirement be ethical? Would it make a difference to how the human resources manager handled this potential conflict of interests, based on whom they consider their client to be – the employee or the company? Would the employee be better placed to make an informed decision about their future if the boundaries and purposes were openly presented? Similarly, how ethical would it be for a counsellor to use counselling skills in order to satisfy the practitioner's personal curiosity or professional development requirements rather than to help the client? Does the client's consent to providing information for these purposes make a difference ethically? How free is a client to withhold consent in the helping relationship if they wish to continue receiving services? Again, is it ethical for a practitioner to use counselling skills to coerce the client into doing something that the practitioner considers will be helpful even though the client is unconvinced or resistant? Furthermore, does it make a difference ethically if the practitioner is striving to prevent the client inflicting irreversible harm on themselves or others? The answer to these questions will be, 'It all depends on the particular circumstances.' Deciding what is ethical can be very problematic in all kinds of helping relationships and will depend on the context, the practitioner's role, the circumstances and the interpretation of those circumstances. Our willingness to grapple with the ethical dimensions of using counselling skills will influence both our clients' and colleagues' opinions about our suitability for this work.

The clients' views of what is ethical are usually a good starting point, especially in roles where the primary purpose is to offer help. The bare bones of clients' ethical expectations are often very simple and eminently reasonable. When we have asked clients about their ethical expectations of users of counselling skills, they have usually replied that the practitioner should be:

- trustworthy
- respectful
- competent
- accountable.

Trustworthiness requires taking account of the risk that the client is taking in seeking help. It also requires protecting personally sensitive information disclosed by clients from being used for purposes other than that for which it was originally disclosed. Ensuring the integrity of the relationship may require checking whether the practitioner and client share the same aims in working together.

Respectfulness requires a willingness to accept and value differences between people and to act in ways that affirm the client as a person worthy of respect. The challenge for the practitioner is striving to understand and accept difference between people rather than rejecting difference too readily or judging what may seem strange as wrong or unacceptable.

Competence presents a considerable challenge in counselling skills. The appropriate and constructive use of the skills is reasonably easily evaluated. The use of the practitioner's sense of him- or herself as a person, the emotional robustness and the depth of knowledge required to assist clients about specific issues can be essential aspects of competence. There is clearly an expectation that practitioners will avoid acting beyond their competence or using the skills primarily as an opportunity to resolve their own problems.

Some form of periodic evaluation and support will help the assessment of competence and its further development. Counsellors have developed a form of consultative support or 'non-managerial' supervision as a way of achieving this. In the corporate sector, mentoring can be a way of accomplishing these aims. Nonetheless it is surprising to the authors that so many caring and helping roles leave practitioners largely unsupported and increasingly subject to periodic authoritative inspections. Such inspections often appear to be more concerned with finding incompetence and deficiency than supporting competence. Teaching, social work and healthcare employ large numbers of personally motivated staff largely unsupported over the difficulties and personal cost of fulfilling their roles. Stress and loss of personal motivation are often the causes of people losing the levels of competence they may have demonstrated earlier in their career.

Accountability to the client involves a willingness to explain how you are working and the reasons for the decisions you have made. In some situations, accountability may extend to colleagues, the funders of services and sometimes other members of the client's family or social network. It is not unusual for accountability to exist in tension with being trustworthy, especially when it involves responsibility beyond the client and raises questions of how to honour the client's confidences. Respect may require that differences in culture are considered in how to be accountable. Some cultures require greater formality or deference by the practitioner than others. Accountability when you consider that you have been incompetent is a test of courage and humility. The use of apology and expression of regret has its place in accountability. We will be turning again to the issues of trust and respect in the next chapter, when we discuss the core conditions that underpin the use of counselling skills.

A more detailed account of the challenges of being ethical in counselling and psychotherapy can be found in *Standards and Ethics for Counselling in Action* (Bond, 2000: 1).

The Learning Process

We have talked about the personal rewards of learning counselling skills. There is often excitement at the beginning and a sense of achievement and fulfilment at the end.

However, what happens in between can be personally challenging. These are not skills that can be learned as impersonal techniques. They impact on both the learner and on existing relationships. Sometimes this will be beneficial; at other times less so. Good counselling skills can be used to help family members and friends with their difficulties, although you may need to be careful about protecting enough space in which you can relate in other ways. Most partners will enjoy some experimentation in how you communicate with them, although as with all experiments the outcome may be unpredictable. Being empathic and using skills to reflect back the important points of what another is saying may forestall an argument, because the other person feels heard. Conversely, it may frustrate them, if they were hoping to learn more of your views and experience or to clear the air with an argument. The issues of selecting the appropriate strategies and skills apply just as much to your social contacts as to your relationships with clients. Generally we like to be more reciprocal and spontaneous with friends and partners than this model envisages us being with clients. In our experience, you will want to be more considered in your responses to clients than might be the case with established relationships.

The emotional response to learning a skill can be surprisingly powerful. Again this can be captured as stages in a cycle:

1   *Unconscious incompetence.* We start the learning cycle in a state of blissful ignorance of how we communicate and respond to other people's problems. We take listening and responding for granted. We have little or no awareness of the potential for improvement.
2   *Conscious incompetence.* This stage marks your beginning consciousness or awareness of how you typically communicate. It is not always a comfortable experience. This stage may be characterised by confusion or by feeling de-skilled. There can be a sense of loss of what had been familiar and unproblematic. There may also be a sense of excitement about new opportunities. However, despite discomfort, this is the turning point where you realise the potential for improvement and look forward to the possibilities offered by new skills.

3   *Conscious competence.* The pursuit of conscious competence will vary in difficulty. Some skills will be relatively easily acquired. Others may be perplexing and difficult to implement. The examples in the book have been chosen to help you familiarise yourself with the skills. You can be greatly helped by having someone who is able to demonstrate them. An experienced tutor in counselling skills is ideal. Alternatively you can use audio and video recordings to supplement this book.

4   *Unconscious competence.* The completion of the cycle is reached as you become sufficiently confident in your competence such that the newly acquired skill forms part of your natural repertoire. The sense of strangeness and artificiality fades. You start to incorporate the new skill seamlessly into your own way of communicating and working, with progressively less and less conscious awareness.

A Continuous Loop

Working in an 'unconsciously' competent way is of course not the end of the story. It is akin to reaching a learning plateau. Discussions in your supervision or the issues that clients bring or events in your own life are some examples of the incidents that might alert you to the need to change aspects of your practice or extend your repertoire of skills. At this point, you will became aware that you have grown into a state of unconscious incompetence, albeit at an improved level – at which point you start the cycle again.

This process will become very familiar to you as you work through this book. In the next chapter we will introduce the model, its structure and stages.

2

OVERVIEW
Introducing the Integrative Skills Model

Using counselling skills is an exciting and complex activity that does not come naturally to most of us. It is something that we learn to do by integrating theory with practice and by reflecting on our work. As with most intricate processes one way to learn is to break the operation down into component parts. Perhaps you can remember learning to swim. You may recall learning first how to kick your legs, before moving on to synchronising arm and leg movements. Your initial efforts were almost certainly ungainly as you tried to time your breathing with the moments when your face was out of the water. Gradually, you became more skilful; you ceased to think about breathing and what to do with your limbs; you became competent in an 'unconscious' way. Your swimming now will be nothing like the component parts. It will have a grace and a fluidity of its own. Just as swimming is more than a collection of bodily movements so, of course, using counselling skills effectively is more than applying a collection of skills. However, developing competency in counselling may be approached by identifying and practising the basic communication skills, integrating them into a model that enables the whole process to be understood, however long it lasts.

This chapter provides you with an overview of the counselling model described in detail in this book. Before outlining the model, we want to discuss briefly the title we have used. The term 'integrative skills' denotes what we think are two key features of the model. Fundamentally, it is skills based, meaning that it has at its core a set of communication skills which each of us needs in order to work effectively with clients. The skills in all their various combinations are the necessary components. We have used the term 'integrative' to signify that these constituent parts have been combined according to some rules or guiding principles. The model provides an organising framework for using counselling skills purposefully and consistently.

Essentially this model provides us with a map of the counselling *process* as distinct from *content*. Content is what clients bring to the interaction – their thoughts, feelings, behaviours and their experiences. Content is the *what*: 'What is this client saying to you both verbally and non-verbally?' All counsellors and practitioners certainly need models for understanding and sorting content with their clients.

The term 'process' refers to the dynamics of the counselling relationship or the *how*; how you and your clients are working together and what is happening between you. Just as we need a model for comprehending content, so we need a conceptual plan for making sense of process. This framework helps us to understand our current interactions with clients – to figure out what has been happening as well as to determine what needs to happen – if the counselling work is to proceed to the desired and agreed conclusion.

Let us now consider the structure of the model.

Stages

The framework we have used is one of stages. Conceptualising counselling and therapy as a series of incremental stages or defined points is common to many approaches and is a way of imposing structure on what otherwise might be a random or chaotic activity (Egan, 2002; Nelson-Jones, 2000; Tolan, 2003). We have simply called the stages Beginning, Middle and Ending because all encounters, however long they last, have a beginning, a middle and an end. We are concerned also with what ideally should happen at each stage. In other words, what outcomes are desirable at various points in the counselling process and what strategies and skills will be effective in attaining them. The process elements are the strategies and skills that you use to give purpose and direction to your counselling. The model attempts to integrate skills into sequences; to incorporate skills into strategies; and to unify the counselling encounter, whether it lasts for one or a number of sessions. To this end, we have identified aims for each stage, together with strategies and skills appropriate for realising these aims. The model therefore provides you with a theoretical template for conducting the counselling work.

Strategies

We use the term strategy to mean a procedure. Using counselling skills ought to be a purposeful activity and you will need to be clear about what you are attempting to do at each stage of the process and to know why you are attempting it. For example, exploration is one of the strategies of the Beginning Stage. You will engage in exploration with clients for several purposes, one of which is to create a clear and mutual understanding of the meaning and significance to clients of their concerns. Some people are greatly helped by exploration alone to the extent that they require no further help. With other clients, exploration may be essential in order to create a basis for offering further help, for example by using other strategies such as goal setting or action planning.

Skills

By counselling skills, we mean competency or accomplishment in communication, acquired or developed in training. The skills outlined in this model are the basic tools by which you put the strategies into operation and fulfil the aims of each stage. For example, paraphrasing is a core counselling skill. It is a way of communicating that you have heard and understood what the client has said. Its value lies in what it enables practitioners to achieve with clients when they use it. Accurate paraphrasing is a key skill for communicating empathic understanding and for relationship building. As such, it is indispensable to the strategy of exploration. It is also one of the core components both for effective challenging and for assessing goals.

Let us look now at the model itself.

Beginning Stage

During the Beginning Stage of the counselling process you will primarily be concerned with relationship building and assessment. We have identified the following four aims to guide the work of this stage. The aims are the intended outcomes or what you want to achieve.

Aims

1 *To establish a working relationship.* This aim is fundamental. The effective use of counselling skills depends on establishing a good working relationship and sustaining it. You will need to develop the kind of relationship in which clients are able to connect with you and feel encouraged to invest energy in working with you. Unless clients believe that you are trustworthy and respectful, they will be unlikely either to ally themselves with you or to allow you to know them in anything more than a superficial way.

2 *To clarify and define problems.* It is reasonable to suppose that, if you and clients are to work together, both of you should understand what issues and concerns clients have. Often clients are unclear about what bothers them or they may have multiple issues to deal with and be uncertain where to start.

3 *To make an assessment.* By this we mean formulating hypotheses about what clients share with you. Two of the assessments you will need to make are whether or not you are likely to be able to assist specific clients and whether or not you are willing to work with them to help them achieve what they want.

4 *To negotiate a contract.* Establishing a contract helps to secure a mutual agreement about how you will work together and thus contributes to establishing the working relationship. The contract provides the guidelines for the work and encompasses both explicit and implicit agreement between you and clients. Contracting is a significant procedure for conveying the notion of your relationship with the client as a shared enterprise and not something that is 'done to' clients by an 'expert'. It is a way of both recognising clients' responsibility for themselves and inviting their cooperation. In some working contexts negotiating a contract is sometimes referred to as 'managing expectations'.

Strategies

The following strategies will enable you to accomplish the aims of the Beginning Stage. Let us briefly consider each in turn.

1 *Exploration* involves helping clients to examine and elucidate their concerns. The purpose is to clarify and to arrive at a shared understanding of the nature of clients' dilemmas.

2   *Prioritising and focusing* means deciding in what order clients will tackle their concerns and identifying what is at the hub of the issues they bring.

3   *Communicating core values* is concerned with demonstrating your acceptance or respect, empathic understanding and genuineness or congruence. The core values, often referred to as the core conditions, are those attitudes and beliefs that form the heart of a counselling relationship (Rogers, 1961, 1980; Mearns and Thorne, 1999, 2000). They are indispensable to developing a relationship of trust, containment and one in which change can be explored. Acceptance is concerned with esteeming clients because they are human, not because of their actions, achievements, skills or appearance. It means respecting difference, prizing uniqueness and distinguishing between the person and the behaviour. Empathic understanding means developing the ability and the willingness to see clients' worlds as they see them. Genuineness testifies to our ability to be open, sincere and visible in the relationship. These values need to permeate the manner in which you respond to clients. Without them the counselling process will lack vibrancy; while the use of the strategies and skills will become perfunctory and weakened in their impact.

4   *Being concrete or specific* deserves a particular mention. We think the ability to be concrete and encourage explicit communication is a composite strategy. It has two aspects concerning awareness and communication. You will of course need to listen 'actively' to what clients are saying and be aware of generalisations, distortions, omissions, and ambiguities. It goes without saying that you will not be in a position to invite a more concrete description if you are oblivious to the vagueness in what clients are saying. Second, you will need to use your communication skills sensitively to encourage appropriate clarity.

Foundation skills

These are the most important basic skills upon which the work of both this and subsequent stages in the counselling process depend. They can be used in a variety of combinations or sequences to put each of the strategies into operation.

1   *Attending and listening.* In order to understand clients and communicate your understanding, you will obviously need to listen to them. We

are using the term 'active listening' to mean listening with purpose and responding in such a way that clients are aware they have been both heard and understood.

We have arranged the ways in which you might respond verbally to clients into two skill clusters, namely *reflective* and *probing*.

2   *Reflective skills*. The starting point for this set of skills is the clients' frame of reference. Their distinguishing feature is capturing what clients are telling you and repeating the message in your own words. Reflective skills are valuable for 'tracking' clients, since they impose minimal direction from the practitioner. Using them enables you to communicate the core values, to clarify and to acknowledge clients' experiences. As such, they are powerful skills for building relationships that are both supportive and challenging. They are also ideal information gathering skills. The reflective skills are:

- *restating* what you believe to be a significant word or phrase that the client has used
- *paraphrasing*, which involves conveying clients' core messages (facts and feelings) in your own words
- *summarising*, which is offering clients a précis of the information they have given you – not as a list of details and facts but as an organised overview of important themes or clusters of concerns.

3   *Probing skills*. The source of the probing skills is invariably the practitioner's view or 'frame of reference'. Whenever you ask a question, you will be focusing on what you want to know and not necessarily what clients want to tell you. As such all questions 'lead' or direct clients. However, probing has an important part to play in counselling. You will need information from clients and at times may want to influence the direction of the exploration. In general, probes are interventions that increase practitioner control over both process and content. For this reason, we think they should be used sparingly and with care, particularly in the early stages of counselling.

The probing skills are:

- *questioning* – in Chapter 3, we describe different types of questions and discuss how questions might both facilitate and inhibit exploration
- *making statements* is a gentler form of probing. For example, instead of asking a client 'What did she do to upset you?', you

might say 'I'm not sure what she did to upset you.' Statements tend to be less intrusive and controlling than questions.

Middle Stage

The Middle Stage focuses on helping clients to reassess or reframe their problems and concerns. This type of reassessment marks the important shift in the process away from problems and towards solutions. Reassessment encourages clients to develop different ways of looking at their problems, ways that are more liberating and support movement towards goals and action. Without these new pictures of themselves and their concerns, clients are unlikely to effect change. Let us look at the aims.

Aims

1 *To reassess problems and concerns.* Clients will have their own views or perspectives on their concerns. Reassessment involves helping them to see themselves from different and more empowering perspectives.
2 *To maintain the working relationship.* This is critical to the whole counselling encounter. Reassessment can be tough for clients. The discoveries they make about themselves and their behaviour often being very painful. One of their ways of handling this discomfort may be to test the strength of their relationship with you and your commitment to them. You will need to be robust enough to 'contain' their anger, distress or disappointment.
3 *To work to the contract.* Contracts may be renegotiated as the counselling progresses. However, you will need to keep the contract in mind throughout. It specifies the purpose that you and clients have agreed at the outset.

Strategies

1 *Challenging* is the means by which clients are helped to develop different and more enabling perspectives on the dilemmas or problems that brought them into counselling. At its best, challenging provokes deeper exploration, by which we mean that clients are encouraged to explore what they have hitherto been unaware of or only dimly aware of, as well as what they may have been avoiding or overlooking. There are specific ways of challenging and each of the following strategies has a specific focus:

- *Confrontation* is effective in helping clients to identify and face the games or ruses which they employ and which inhibit change.
- *Giving feedback* involves letting clients know how you experience them and their behaviour.
- *Giving information* can encourage clients to assess themselves and their situations differently.
- *Giving directives* means openly directing the process. When, for example, you instruct a client to, 'Say to me what you wanted to say to her', you will be directing them to experience something different. This different experience is intended to provide some insight into how they thought about, and behaved in, the situation under discussion or what their inhibitions are about tackling a specific concern with a colleague.
- *Self-disclosure or self-sharing* means talking about your own experiences. Used sparingly, it has the effect of freeing clients to explore their own concerns in a more open and meaningful way.
- *Immediacy* focuses both on the relationship between you and on what is happening now. Being immediate means offering clients your perspective on the interaction between you and encouraging them to reflect on what is happening.

2 *Communicating core values.* Clients are more likely to be open to challenges and use the invitation to explore more deeply if they feel safe enough with you. This sense of safety will usually be related to the degree to which clients experience you as accepting of them, respectful of their endeavours, trustworthy and congruent.

Skills

The foundation skills identified in the Beginning Stage provide the basis for the more complex challenging strategies deployed in the Middle Stage. You will use them in sequences or combinations to influence clients to look afresh at their concerns.

Ending Stage

The Ending Stage typically has to do with planning for and taking effective action. It also focuses on ending the counselling relationship.

Aims

1 *To decide on appropriate change.* If clients are to make changes, then they will need to know what changes are possible and what particular outcomes they want.
2 *To implement change.* Change involves taking some action. Clients may need help to act. For example, talking about expressing anger appropriately is not the same as doing it.
3 *To transfer learning.* If clients are to succeed in coping with their concerns, what they learn in counselling about their behaviour and the different options open to them will need to be transferred to their life outside the counselling room.
4 *To end the working relationship.* A sense of relationship will have grown from your clients meeting and sharing with you as well as being supported by you and experiencing your commitment. It will have been a very important relationship for most clients. Ending is concerned with recognising the loss of this relationship as well as the fulfilment of a contract.

Strategies

1 *Goal setting.* Goal setting provides a framework and a set of criteria which will enable you to identify and to assess with clients the outcomes they say they want. It is an adaptable strategy that allows for the integration of different techniques, for example scaling, guided fantasy, rehearsal and role-play.
2 *Action planning.* If clients are to act, then ideally they need to choose from all the available options open to them and to plan their action.
3 *Evaluating action and sustaining change.* Action needs to be reviewed and evaluated. The important question for clients is 'Is this action helping me to cope better with my concerns?' Reviewing will also be concerned with the sustainability of the action.
4 *Ending.* Reviewing the work and helping clients to identify and own the changes they have made is part of this strategy. Clients may need time and space to work through their feelings of sadness and loss. During the ending stage, it is not unusual for clients to become anxious about leaving a supportive relationship.

Skills

Again, the foundation skills are the communication part of the above strategies.

This model, of course, provides a static picture of what is usually experienced as a complex, fluid and changing process. Counselling skills in action are not a neat, linear operation with a defined structure and discrete stages. It is much more complicated and subtle, with both client and practitioner working in their own unique ways. The model, therefore, simply represents a plan for you. It is neither a description of how clients actually behave nor of what counselling is.

However, conceptualising counselling as a series of stages is an attempt to introduce some stable points into the process. These will be points at which the work begins to change by adopting a different focus. The model provides guidance about not only what to do at each stage but also how and when to do it. Implicit in its structure is the idea that certain things should precede others. For example, goals should precede action, otherwise the action may be misdirected. Using this model and being aware of your intentions as well as developing your skills by practising, so that you communicate what you actually intend to communicate, seems to us a responsible way to approach counselling and of using counselling skills.

In one sense, this is a meta-model for using counselling skills because it can be integrated with other theoretical approaches. Whatever theory you espouse, you will need the strategies and the skills with which to implement that theory. Just as practitioners need theories that attempt both to explain how individuals have developed as they have and to provide models of healthy development, so they need frameworks to understand process. This model conceptualises process and enables you to translate theory into practice.

Its strength is that it provides a clear, sensible and accessible framework for practitioners. However, like any framework, unless it is used sensitively and flexibly, it will tyrannise rather than liberate the users.

To conclude this overview, we want to outline some of the basic assumptions about the nature of people and the nature of change that underpins this model.

Basic Assumptions

The way you work, the frameworks and interventions you choose, can be said to be a reflection of your values and assumptions about people, about counselling and the change process. For example, if we repeatedly tell clients what to do, our behaviour could be said to be a reflection of our belief that they are not capable of making their own choices and need an expert to guide them. Each of us will have principles, however embryonic, that guide and inform our practice. Becoming clear and explicit about beliefs and basic assumptions means that they are available as 'anchors' in the midst of confusion. Being aware of our guiding values also means they are open to examination, challenge and modification as a result of our experiences with clients.

Here are some of the assumptions:

1 *People deserve acceptance and understanding because they are human.* This means that you will make a distinction between the clients themselves and their behaviour. While you will strive to communicate to them that you value them as individuals, it does not mean that you will necessarily value or condone their behaviour.

2 *People are capable of change.* Clients have learned ways of behaving which do not serve them well. They can identify and develop different ways of responding both to their problems and to others. Given a supportive environment, where trying out new ideas does not carry the risk of rejection or ridicule, they will be capable of discovering options for more satisfying behaviour.

3 *People create their own meaning.* What seems chaotic or unhelpful to us will have some meaning for clients. They may be involved to varying degrees in the creation of their own misery by the way they interpret, react to and try to make sense of events and experiences. For example, clients who believe they are 'failures' may confirm that view to themselves by setting goals that they cannot hope to achieve, construing success as luck and disregarding positive feedback. They are interpreting their experiences to fit their often long-held and 'safe' views of themselves and their worlds. Counselling, with its focus on awareness and change, provides a challenge to the meaning that clients' attribute to their experiences and helps them to risk a different and more enlivening interpretation.

4 *People are experts on themselves.* Clients know best how they feel and what they believe and think. They, better than anyone, can tell what the pain and disappointments are like for them, what their fears are and what they most want for themselves. However, they may need varying amounts of help to do that. Clients may have had a lifetime of being told what they want, what is best for them and what they feel.

5 *People have the desire to realise their potential.* Clients are often clients because they want to become more self-directing and more self-empowered. They have the potential to get past the blocks of self-sabotage and discover what is right for them, if they are given the climate in which to make that discovery. They have the ability to think for themselves and have the resources to deal in more creative ways with their problems and concerns.

6 *People's behaviour is purposeful.* However undermining clients' behaviour appears both to them and to you, thinking about it as having a rationale and being directed towards some outcome is a valuable starting point in helping them to gain some insight into their actions. Clients' behaviour can be understood in terms of the purposes that it serves for them, although the result may be the very outcome they are attempting to avoid.

7 *People will work harder to achieve goals which they value and which they have set for themselves.* Individuals are more likely to marshal their resources and struggle for outcomes that they want, rather than goals that are imposed. Helping clients to identify the outcomes they want is a significant aspect of the counselling process.

Let us now turn to the model in detail and begin with the foundation skills that underpin all aspects of using counselling strategies and skills.

3

THE FOUNDATION SKILLS

This chapter is concerned with skills. We have used the term 'foundation' to describe these skills because not only are they appropriate for accomplishing the work of the early stages of counselling help, but they also form the basis of the more complex strategies; those that are more typically used later on in the helping process. To describe skills as 'foundation' or 'basic' does not imply that their use is restricted to the beginning of the work or that they are undemanding competencies which have little place in later and perhaps more intense episodes. Proficiency in these skills, which will be used in different combinations or sequences to achieve a range of aims, is critical. We begin by discussing *attending* and *listening* and continue with *reflective* and *probing* skills.

Attending Skills

Attending and listening are interrelated skills that both complement and affect each other. It is not possible to attend fully to clients without listening to them. Conversely, attending well to clients places you in a good position to listen to them, to both their verbal and non-verbal messages (Egan, 2002). We have separated them here for the purpose of analysis and discussion, although the division is theoretical.

Attending acts as a basis for listening to and observing clients. It is the means by which you communicate 'non-verbally' that you are 'with them', interested in them and alert to what they want to share with you. The manner in which you attend to clients will carry powerful messages, and the effect of what you say to them will be diminished if your non-verbal behaviour is at variance with your words (Argyle, 1988). Communicating acceptance, understanding and genuineness will be enhanced if you attend well.

Let us look briefly at some of the ways you can show that you are attending to clients:

1 *Posture.* Your posture needs to be 'open'. In other words to signal that you are receptive to and willing to engage with clients. Find a position that is comfortable, face the client directly, sit in a centred way, upright and yet relaxed. Leaning back in your chair is unlikely to communicate alert attention.

2 *Eye contact.* You will be concerned to maintain constant and direct eye contact. This does not mean fixing clients with a stare, but rather using eye contact to demonstrate your availability. In other words, whenever clients return their gaze to you, they will find you looking at them. Argyle (1988) suggests that, if clients are looking and sounding uncomfortable, then breaking eye contact temporarily can be helpful in enabling them to continue with difficult issues. Your aim will be to maintain a natural pattern of eye contact that communicates your interest in the other person.

3 *Facial expression.* As you will be observing your clients so they will be watchful of you. You will need to be aware of the information that your facial expression might convey. How you look should, of course, be consistent or congruent with what you are saying. You may also want to mirror clients by matching your expression with theirs. For example, by looking pleased with them when they report success. Mirroring also encourages exploration in a non-intrusive way – for example, clients may reveal extremely painful material to you in an unemotional and detached way. Letting clients see, by the concern on your face, that you have some sense of the pain and misery they have experienced may free them to begin to access those feelings.

4 *Seating.* You need to ensure that you are seated at an appropriate distance (3–5 ft) and that the chairs are of an equal height. If you are working with a couple, ensure that each of you can look at the others with ease. Sitting at a slight angle, rather than positioning yourself directly opposite appears more relaxed and less confrontational. Making 'space' for clients means providing an appropriate physical environment as well as a supportive relationship and uninterrupted time.

Attending to clients is a way of giving them your presence. If your attending behaviour could speak, it should say: 'I am interested in you and what you have to say. I am ready and willing to work with you and I am genuinely concerned to understand you and your experiences. However awful what you tell me is, I will not buckle under the weight of it.'

Before discussing listening skills, we want to say a few words about observing clients.

Observing clients

As we stated in the previous section, attending to clients puts you in a good position to observe them. They too will be communicating non-verbally. The way they are dressed, their tone of voice, their gestures and postures will either confirm or emphasise or conflict with their verbal messages. Observing clients carefully will help you to develop your understanding of them. You will learn to interpret the clues and cues that they give. For example, you will discover that, while one client smiles when she is hurt, another narrows her eyes and talks angrily.

Focusing on the incongruities and inconsistencies between clients' verbal and non-verbal behaviour facilitates exploration. Clients may not be aware either of what they are feeling or the significance of their feelings. Your timing needs to be sensitive and you need to offer your observations in a tentative way rather than telling or informing. Consider the following examples:

> CLIENT A: [*in a flat voice, looking round the room and sighing*] Yes, I was pleased when she asked me if she could stay for three months. I get on well with my mother.
>
> PRACTITIONER: I notice that your voice sounded flat and I wonder what the sigh was saying.
>
> CLIENT A: [*looking embarrassed*] Well, I suppose it was saying I *was* pleased and, this will sound awful, but now she's beginning to get on my nerves, and I wish she'd go.

and

> CLIENT B: [*loudly, talking quickly and in a harsh tone*] I was frustrated. He shouldn't have spoken to me like that; in front of other people.
>
> PRACTITIONER: Your voice and tone suggest more than irritation to me. You sound very angry.

CLIENT B: Yes, just talking about it, I can feel the anger rising in me. I was so angry, I just walked off. I couldn't speak.

In both examples, the practitioner specifies what she notices and invites the clients to explore the apparent incongruities between their verbal and non-verbal messages. In the first example, the practitioner focused on the *confused* message the client was giving, while, in the second, she attempted to help the client experience the *depth* of his feeling.

It is not our intention to imply that certain postures or gestures have certain meanings, but rather that they mean something. What you will have observed is a piece of behaviour, the meaning and significance of which is available to the client. You will need to watch out for consistent patterns; for example, you may notice that a client has several times broken eye contact when discussing job security, and register your hunches about the meaning or significance. You will seek evidence from other aspects of their behaviour that either supports or disconfirms your hunches. When you sense that there is enough trust between you, you may want to share your observations. Hunches should be shared with clients in a tentative manner. Your purpose in sharing will be to encourage clients to further exploration and greater self-understanding. Observations that are offered as 'facts' or interpretations as to the meaning of certain aspects of behaviour typically help to create resistance.

We have somewhat artificially separated non-verbal behaviour into practitioner's and client's. Non-verbal communication is of course dynamic. You and your clients will be reacting to the clues that pass between you at both a conscious and an unconscious level. Any discussion of their non-verbal behaviour should usefully include a discussion of yours. You may have been inviting the very behaviour from clients about which you are concerned. A simple example will illustrate this point. A trainee interviewer complained that he had experienced difficulty in establishing rapport with a client because the client was so anxious and hesitant. A video recording of the interview revealed that, as soon as the client started talking, the interviewer began to take notes. This had the effect of him breaking eye-contact and turning away from her. Deprived of cues, the client became hesitant and eventually stopped talking.

Finally, we are an increasingly diverse, multicultural and multi-ethnic society. Developing cultural as well as individual empathy will help you to work sensitively with clients whose patterns of non-verbal (and verbal) expression may be very different from yours; and who may also have expectations that are at variance with your notions of what constitutes counselling support (Ponterotto et al., 1995; Lago and Smith, 2003).

Let us turn now to listening.

Listening Skills

Listening is a complex activity and a skill that operates on many levels. It involves attending to, receiving and understanding the messages that clients are sending both by what they say and by what they do. Your purpose in listening will be to facilitate understanding between you and them and to reach a common agreement about both what concerns them and how they experience their concerns. However, when you are listening to them, you are not a sponge soaking up the information indiscriminately. The amount of information passing between you will be too great for you to pick up and respond to every cue and clue. Therefore, you will be doing several things: you will be sorting the information and deciding what to respond to; you will be forming hypotheses about what they are saying as well as what they are omitting; and you will be seeking clarification of aspects which are unclear. In other words, you will be listening 'actively'. 'Active listening' means that you are listening with purpose *and* communicating that you have listened. Ways of responding to clients will be discussed in the next section. However, in order to focus your listening, we want to outline one framework

A framework for listening

The following framework offers a simple and useful system for classifying the information that clients share with you:

- *Experiences* – what clients experience as happening to them; what others do or fail to do; what others say or do not say.
- *Behaviour* – how clients act; what they say and do.
- *Feelings* – what they feel about their behaviour and their experiences.
- *Thoughts* – what clients understand about what they do or do not do; what sense they make of their own and others' behaviour; and what beliefs they have about themselves, other people and events in their lives.

This framework will assist you in your analysis of the interview process. For example, you may be aware that your client talks easily about what he does and what he thinks about his own and others' behaviour. He does not express feelings easily or make many feeling statements. You may decide to intervene to encourage him to get in touch with his feelings, in order to help him to gain greater self- understanding.

Listening to silences

Communication between you and clients will continue even if one or both of you are silent. Silence can be a potent way of 'speaking volumes' and you will need to listen to their silences as well as their words. By attending carefully in sessions, you will gain some clues about what they might be thinking and feeling when they are silent. For example, you will discern whether they are uneasy, 'stuck', bored, hostile or reflecting. Using that information will help you to decide when and how to intervene. Some practitioners say that they avoid interrupting silences and routinely wait for clients to continue. That seems a sensible strategy. However, too rigidly applied, it may mean that some clients are not helped to proceed. On the other hand, if you are invariably the one who breaks silences, you may want to explore that in supervision. It could be that, by inviting clients to talk, you are making the time more congenial for yourself. Listening to and using silences creatively in using counselling skills means effecting an appropriate balance between:

- enabling clients
- providing space for them to reflect
- helping them to face their discomfort.

The following example illustrates how you might break a silence.

The client, who has been exploring a work issue for a couple of minutes in a desultory way, stops and gazes out of the window. She begins to look sad and her eyes water. The silence lasts for a couple of minutes.

PRACTITIONER: I wonder what you are thinking about.

CLIENT: Oh! Nothing much!

PRACTITIONER: You look sad and your eyes were becoming misty.

CLIENT: Well! That's odd, because if you want to know, I was thinking about the shopping I was doing before I came here today. I raced around looking for a present. I found it so difficult to choose something. I've got something but I'm not satisfied with it. I don't think it will be quite right.

PRACTITIONER: So what you eventually chose won't be good enough, is that it?

CLIENT: [*starting to cry*] Yes, whatever I do, however hard I try, I just won't get it right. My efforts won't be good enough. That's how I feel a lot of the time. I'm not good enough.

Here the practitioner broke the silence by giving specific feedback on what she observed and using paraphrasing to prompt the client to explore. She responded to the client's verbal and non-verbal messages. In doing so, she encouraged her to focus on a fundamental issue to do with her beliefs about her self-worth.

Interrupting silences

In addition to giving specific feedback, you might also 'break' silences by asking 'process' questions. For example:

'What are you feeling now?'
'What are you thinking?'
'What's going on for you at the moment?'
'What's happening?'

'Process' questions, although direct, are much less intrusive than 'content' questions. They also keep your focus on the client's current experiences.

Listening to your reactions

As you listen to clients, you will be thinking, feeling and intuiting. Listening to your own reactions may provide valuable clues both to understanding what is happening in sessions and to understanding clients themselves. For example, you may be aware that you are irritated with a client and begin to pay close attention to what happens between you when you feel irritated. You may at an appropriate time share this and invite exploration. It may be that your response helps her to understand others' reactions to her behaviour and that this is how her relationships become distant and dissatisfying. Paying close attention to the patterns of your reactions to clients and their material is the basis for behaving congruently. Mearns and Thorne (1999) provide some valuable guidelines for sharing thoughts and feelings with a client.

Listening filters

None of us listens in a completely disinterested way. We all have filters through which information from clients passes. The frameworks we use to organise information from them will inevitably introduce bias by filtering out certain aspects of the interaction. Some of the major obstacles to active listening are:

1   *Culture*. A knowledge of your own and others' culture will certainly assist your listening to and understanding of clients. This is particularly important when working with clients from different cultural backgrounds. However, cultural norms and values are the most difficult to transcend. It may mean that you discuss the possibility of helping some clients to find practitioners who share their cultural backgrounds or discuss with them how they feel and what they think about working with someone who is from a different cultural background. For further discussion see Pedersen et al. (1996); Lago and Thompson (1996); and d'Ardenne and Mahtani (1999) in the 'Counselling in Action' series.
2   *Values*. It is important that we be aware of our own values and, in so far as it is possible, that we refrain from imposing them on our clients, either overtly or covertly. Ethical considerations apart, we need to rid ourselves of beliefs about the way clients should conduct their lives.
3   *Issues in the practitioner's life*. Most of us at some time or another have difficulties in our own lives that preoccupy us and render us less open to others. To be effective means being able to suspend your concerns and create space for clients.

Other hindrances to active listening arise from:

- Preparing your reply to what the client is saying.
- Seeking confirmation for your hypotheses and ignoring information from the client which contradicts these hypotheses.
- Either becoming defensive or labelling yourself inadequate when clients attempt to correct you.
- Being anxious about what the client is telling you.

- Trying to find a solution, because by temperament you are 'action orientated'.

Listening attentively, with an awareness of the filters you have and the issues in your own life, is the basis for understanding clients. However, while listening is important, it is not enough. Clients need more. They need you to respond in order to know that they are being heard and understood. Let us now discuss the skills of reflecting and probing as ways of responding verbally to clients.

Reflective Skills

Reflective skills are skills that enable you to communicate your understanding of the client's perspective or frame of reference. This is sometimes referred to as understanding the *internal frame of reference* or how clients view themselves and their concerns. Probing skills, on the other hand, usually express the practitioner's perspective or *external frame of reference* (Nelson-Jones, 2000). When you probe, you will be responding from your frame of reference. You will usually do this when seeking information or wanting to influence the direction of a session.

We consider reflective skills to be the single most useful group of skills in the repertoire. They are without equal for building trust and for encouraging exploration as well as for discouraging premature focusing. They provide a medium for communicating empathic understanding and acceptance in a way in which the probing skills do not. Using reflective skills will enable you to 'track' clients' thinking and feeling; to check in a non-intrusive way that you have understood; and to impose minimal direction from your frame of reference. The common element in these skills is offering back to clients what they have said using your own words.

The three reflective skills are:

1   restating
2   paraphrasing
3   summarising.

We will discuss each of them in turn.

Restating

Restating involves repeating back to clients either single words or short phrases which they have used. It is an efficient way of prompting further discussion. Consider the following example:

> CLIENT: I felt *so punished.*
> PRACTITIONER: Punished? [*restating*]
> CLIENT: Yes, I put thought and effort into that essay and the feedback was so cutting. I felt really down. I thought it deserved a higher mark too. I don't trust my judgement any more.

The practitioner restated a word that was both emphasised and emotionally loaded. It encouraged further response and enabled the practitioner to stay with the client's frame of reference. It provided minimal direction to the client and was not as intrusive as a question – for example, 'What do you mean by punished?' This kind of restating is often referred to as a 'one-word' question because the practitioner typically adopts an enquiring tone.

Restating is also a useful skill for maintaining the focus in a session. For example:

> CLIENT: I felt like a fish out of water. I didn't know anyone. That doesn't usually matter. Oh! Actually I did know someone but he was so involved with other people . . . Where was I?
> PRACTITIONER: Feeling like a fish out of water?
> CLIENT: I felt so out of it – so lacking in confidence. I thought 'I'm not as interesting as other people.' Here I go again, putting myself down.

The practitioner's intention here was to remind the client of what she was saying and encourage her to continue.

Take care not to overuse restating. Consider the following example, in which the practitioner only restates the client's words:

> CLIENT: I felt *so miserable.*
> PRACTITIONER: Miserable.
> CLIENT: Yes, and depressed. I wonder if I'll ever feel happy again sometimes.
> PRACTITIONER: Happy?
> CLIENT: Well, settled in a relationship.

The interview sounds stilted and contrived. Restating provides an economical way of encouraging clients. However, practitioners need a mix of skills. Using one to the exclusion of others is tedious, sounds false and may well irritate clients.

Paraphrasing

Paraphrasing is the skill of rephrasing what you understand to be the core message of the client's communication. It is letting clients know that you understand their concerns from their points of view. The frame of reference for paraphrasing is the client's. Your intentions in using this skill will be:

1 *To check your perception of what clients have said.* Paraphrasing allows both you and clients to know whether or not you are both sharing a common understanding of their problems.
2 *To communicate the core qualities of acceptance and empathic understanding.* Developing proficiency in this skill is a key way of letting clients know that you are with them and concerned to see their point of view. However, paraphrasing is not the same as accepting and understanding clients. Without congruence, paraphrasing will sound formulaic and far from empathic. Nonetheless, attending to clients well enough to paraphrase accurately puts you in an excellent position both to accept and to understand them.
3 *To gain information about how clients see themselves and their concerns.* Paraphrasing is an excellent information-gathering skill because it allows you to follow clients without imposing a direction. It gives them room to say what is important for them. Of course, you may certainly have occasion to ask them for information and to direct the session at some points; and we will be discussing ways of doing this in the section on the probing skills.
4 *To build a trusting relationship.* Clients often feel ashamed and vulnerable. They may wonder if they can trust you to treat them with seriousness and respect. Paraphrasing is a way of receiving what they bring in a manner free of judgement and evaluation.

To be effective, paraphrasing must, of course, be accurate. You would hardly be communicating good understanding if most of what you offered a client was incorrect or 'off the mark'. Developing the skill involves both attending well and listening accurately. It also means being open to clients and their experiences and genuinely wanting to understand them.

Paraphrasing is a key skill in achieving the aims of the Beginning Stage because of the powerful way it allows you to respond in an accepting and non-judgemental way. It also allows clients to 'hear again' what they have said to you, providing them with the opportunity to understand and to modify what they have just communicated. The following example illustrates the skill in operation.

The client, Lynne, is talking about her home background and how she sees herself.

LYNNE: I suppose I've always felt a failure. I didn't go to university like my brother and I'm not in such a high-powered job. Everything he's done has turned out well. He's successful with minimal effort whereas I've had to work hard to get where I am.

PRACTITIONER: You're comparing your achievements with your brother's and telling yourself you're a failure.

LYNNE: Yes! Sort of not quite first class, you know. In my family he's the high flier; I'm just a plodder. Don't get me wrong, I'm pleased with some of the things I've achieved. I've got a flat, a job and a car but . . . [looking sad]

PRACTITIONER: You sound sad. It's like you're saying 'My achievements aren't good enough.'

LYNNE: I don't think they are. I suppose I think I should have done better. Still it's easy, if you've had everything given to you on a plate, isn't it?

PRACTITIONER: You're angry because, the way you see it, your brother's had it easy.

LYNNE: Yes . . . [bitterly] I feel angry and put upon. My brother's had everything – support – encouragement. My mother actually said the other day that it's always easier for the second child. That's him. I paved the way, fought the battles.

PRACTITIONER: You're resentful of the help he was given.

The practitioner uses paraphrasing to follow the client and to communicate her understanding. She also encourages the client to express her feelings.

Paraphrasing will also enable you to become closely involved with clients but not get hooked into argument or collusion. It is especially useful for receiving strong feelings or attacks from clients without becoming defensive. Consider the following example:

> CLIENT: [*in a furious voice*] It's all right for you. What do you know about failure? You've never been dumped or rejected. All you have to do is sit there and listen. I'm the one who's in the middle of this bloody mess.
>
> PRACTITIONER: You're angry that I'm not able to share what you are going through.
>
> CLIENT: *You* bet I am! With you, with my ex-husband. Oh! with everything!
>
> PRACTITIONER: And I really don't know what life is like for you.
>
> CLIENT: *No!* [*slowly and quietly*] I guess no one can really and that's difficult for me.

Finally, paraphrasing is an excellent skill for helping clients to clarify for themselves what they mean. In order for you to understand clients, they also have to understand themselves. For example:

> CLIENT: I'm useless! I've been dithering all week. I can't make up my mind whether to take the job or not. Sometimes I think I'd be mad not to take it. At other times, I think it isn't what I want.
>
> PRACTITIONER: You're undecided. Now you've got the job, you're not sure you want it.
>
> CLIENT: [*pausing*] Well! Now I hear you say that, I realise I do want the job. But I'm not sure I ought to take it. I'm scared of not succeeding in it. I don't want to fail.

This client, hearing the practitioner's paraphrase, realised that what she said was not what she meant.

Guidelines for paraphrasing

1   Be tentative and offer your perception of what the client has said.
2   Avoid telling, informing or defining for the client.
3   Be respectful – do not judge, dismiss or use sarcasm.
4   Use your own words; repeating verbatim is not paraphrasing and may seem like mimicry.
5   Listen to the depth of feeling expressed by the client and match the level in your response.
6   Do not add to what the client says, evaluate it or offer interpretations.

7   Be congruent and don't pretend you understand. You might say something like, 'I want to understand. Let me check with you . . .'
8   Be brief and direct.
9   Keep your voice tone level. Paraphrasing in a shocked or disbelieving tone of voice is unlikely to communicate either acceptance or empathy.

Summarising

Summaries are essentially longer paraphrases. Using them enables you to bring together salient aspects of the session in an organised way. The summaries you will be offering in the initial stages may be called 'attending summaries'. These summaries focus on what the client has said and do not include sharing your hypotheses. The most useful attending summaries are those which give some coherence and order to what the client has been saying and provide an overview to the work so far. Let us consider two possible summaries that the practitioner might make in her session with Lynne.

> PRACTITIONER: From what you've said so far, you seem to feel resentful and angry about the way in which you were treated unfairly by your parents. You also compare yourself unfavourably with your brother and see your achievements as inferior to his.

> PRACTITIONER: You have talked a lot about competition with your brother and how your battles seemed to pave the way forward for him. You are also concerned that you haven't done as well as your parents expected.

In each summary, the practitioner attempts both to review and organise the core content of the session so far. Summarising is a useful way to:

1   *Clarify content and feelings.* Clients often present complicated issues and concerns. Also, clients in distress do not usually organise or package their problems neatly for the practitioner's benefit. You will want to be sure that you have grasped the salient points. You may need to check that you are following the client as accurately as you imagine you are. You might say something like: 'I'd like to check that I understand you', and then summarise what you think the client has said.
2   *Review the work.* Summarising is a way of taking stock, which gives clients opportunities either to correct any misunderstandings, or to add to or to reconsider what they have said.

3   *End a session.* In your ending summary, in addition to rounding off the session, you may confirm what the client has agreed to do prior to the next session or what she says she wants to continue to explore in the subsequent session.

4   *Begin a further session.* Summaries are useful for facilitating the opening of a session because they have the effect of bringing you and the client to a common starting point. For example:

> PRACTITIONER: I have been thinking about our last session. We talked mainly about how trapped you seem to be, at work, in your relationship. I wonder whether you would like to continue with that theme or are there other issues you would like to focus on today?

Summaries such as these need to be offered tentatively, otherwise you may set the agenda for the session. Using a summary in this way, however, can be helpful in providing a link between sessions.

5   *Prioritise and focus.* Clients need varying amounts of help to identify what the salient issues are for them and to order priorities. The frameworks for listening and for organising content will enable you to 'listen actively' with the purpose of assisting clients to do this. During each stage of the process you will be receiving much information from clients; for example, how they see themselves and their concerns and how they view others. You will be forming hypotheses about what they are saying and what they are omitting. You will be identifying patterns and themes as well as the 'maps' that they use to make sense of their worlds.

6   *Move the helping process forward.* In order to move forward, you will need to make some judgements about what direction the conversation might take. In a sense, all the skills, appropriately used, will be instrumental in 'moving' the interview along. However, there will be times when you will want to move forward by introducing a focus to the work. The focus may be for the total encounter, for example when making a contract, or for a specific session or for the next ten minutes.

We now consider two specific types of summary, which are useful for focusing, prioritising and moving the exploration towards making a contract. They are called 'forming a choice point' and 'gaining a figure–ground perspective' (Gilmore, 1973). As you will see, in each case the practitioner attempts to paraphrase the client's point of view while organising the information.

Forming a choice point

There will be times in sessions when you will be able to identify themes or clusters of concerns or different facets to an issue that a client is exploring. Given that clients invariably do have multiple concerns and will need to decide in which order they will tackle them, formulating a choice point is a way of helping clients to make that choice. It involves identifying various aspects or themes by using an attending summary and then asking the client to make a conscious choice about which issue to focus on. Consider the following example:

> CLIENT: [*exploring her concerns about work*] I'm really dissatisfied with the way things are. I don't feel stretched. Well, I am stretched in the sense that I have far too much grinding and boring administrative detail to attend to; but not in the sense of developing my potential. When I mentioned this to my boss, she said 'The details have to be got right. They're the most important things.' I feel stuck and ignored by her. I want her to listen to what I say. If what I'm doing is *so* important, why aren't I paid more and taken notice of?
>
> PRACTITIONER: If I understand correctly, it seems that there are three aspects to your concerns about work: not being stretched and challenged; feeling bored and overloaded with clerical tasks; and not being able to communicate as well as you would like with your boss. Which would be useful for us to focus on?
>
> CLIENT: Talking to my boss, I think. If I could get her backing for some of my ideas, then I'd be freed up to do more interesting work. As it is, all my attempts to talk to her end in stalemate. I don't understand what happens. I leave every conversation with her feeling frustrated, and saying to myself, 'What's the use?'

The practitioner's summary organised the content of the session and identified three aspects to the client's concern. She was tentative and offered the client the choice of where to begin by using an open question. The focus for the work was then agreed.

There may be times when you will want to negotiate with clients about which issue to deal with first. You may think that they are avoiding important issues or you may genuinely believe that it would be appropriate to start elsewhere. However, most times the choice will be that of the client.

Gaining a figure–ground perspective

In this type of summary, the practitioner offers her perception of what she thinks is the most prominent issue for the client. It may be something that the client talks about with heightened emotion or returns to repeatedly. The practitioner may also hypothesise that one issue stands out as the 'crux', and if that issue were managed more productively, then the client would have energy available to tackle other concerns. The notion of figure and ground means that, if one aspect of a client's concerns is in the forefront of his or her awareness or thinking, then other aspects provide a backdrop or are in the background. What comes to the fore may vary and change. Sometimes clients are not aware of the emphases that they are placing on certain issues. Consider the following example:

CLIENT: [*talking about feeling stressed*] I feel pulled in so many directions at the moment – very torn. My mother is elderly and has got noticeably frailer over the last couple of years. Last week she fell. She didn't hurt herself badly but was frightened. We all were. I wonder how long she can manage on her own and I think she'd like to come and live with us. My partner doesn't want that and to be honest neither do I. I've just got promotion to a job I've worked hard for and that I'm determined to succeed in. So, that's another pressure. The new job also means more travelling. It's all change and adjustment. Some of it's positive, like the job; some aspects are frightening, like my mother coming to live with us.

PRACTITIONER: It seems that of all the changes and new demands you're facing now, the one that you anticipate with most concern is caring for your mother. You sounded anxious when you talked about her. I wonder if that is how it seems to you.

CLIENT: Yes, she's really on my mind. I wanted this new job and I know I can cope with the demands it will make. I'd feel more peaceful, if I knew I had some options for looking after Mum and I wasn't so torn.

PRACTITIONER: Would that be useful to look at today? To explore your ideas and fears about looking after your mother?

The practitioner used a short summary to offer her understanding of what was the most prominent concern for the client. From there, she began to negotiate a contract for the session.

Other ways you might introduce a figure–ground perspective are:

- 'What seems to be at the heart of your concerns is . . .'
- 'What stands out for me in what you've been saying is . . .'
- 'One aspect which is becoming clearer to me is . . .'
- 'I'm very aware of . . .'

Remember, it is important to offer your ideas tentatively and to invite clients to comment. They may want to disagree with you and you will need to be willing to explore their different views openly and non-defensively.

In this section, we have reviewed the reflective skills. These skills provide the practitioner with some of the most non-intrusive tools for encouraging clients to explore, clarify and focus. It is impossible not to be directive in using counselling skills. What you see as the core concern for a client and what you choose to reflect back, as well as what you leave or disregard, are all ways in which you influence both direction and content. However, in the initial stages of using counselling skills, when you are getting to know clients, you will seek to create space for them to say what they want with the minimum imposition of your perspective. The reflective skills will assist you in that purpose.

We now consider the probing skills.

Probing Skills

In this section, the probing skills will be identified and their uses and possible effects considered. Probing, as the term suggests, is invasive and – as a trainee once remarked – 'We should use these skills with care; we may be going into areas where we haven't been invited.'

Probes declare the practitioner's perception of what is important to address. When using probes, the control over *content* is shifted away from client to practitioner; the practitioner becomes relatively more directive than when reflecting, paraphrasing or summarising. This is neither wrong nor inadvisable, if probes are used sensitively and judiciously. However, a practitioner who 'specialises' in probing may invite client passivity or appear interrogative. Nonetheless, probing is an important skill. Without it sessions have the potential to become vague or directionless. There will be occasions when it is appropriate to gain information from clients and encourage them to be specific. You may want to direct them to areas that you think are important to explore further. The probing skills of questioning and making statements will now be considered in some detail.

Questioning

We will first look at types of questions before going on to consider both their possible effects and how to ask questions.

Open questions

These are useful forms of questions both for eliciting information and encouraging clients' involvement. Open questions demand a fuller response than 'yes/no' answers. They generally begin with 'what', 'where', 'how' and 'who'. For example, to a client who is talking about arguments with her partner, you might ask:

'What usually happens when you argue?' or
'How do your arguments typically begin?' or
'When do you usually argue?' or
'Where do you argue?' (is it at home? while shopping?) or
'Who is usually the first to want to make up?'

Avoid asking questions that are *too open*. For example, a trainee interviewer was heard to ask a client at the beginning of a session, 'What sort of a person would you say you are?' Questions that are too broad are very difficult to answer. They may faze clients or put unnecessary pressure on them to come up with an answer rather than explore.

Hypothetical questions

As the description suggests these are questions that invite clients to hypothesise and to become explicit about what they imagine or fantasise. They are open questions that invite clients to speculate about future outcomes, and the potential impact of their own and others' behaviours. The fantasies and fears that clients have can be debilitating and often instrumental in preventing them from changing. Not unsurprisingly, clients behave as though what they *fantasise* will definitely happen.

Hypothetical questions are useful for helping clients to articulate their fears and explore them in the relative safety of the helping relationship. Once they put some words to their fears and beliefs, they are available for adjustment. Consider the following example in which the client is complaining of feeling 'put upon' by a friend:

CLIENT: She owes me money from about two months ago and I know I ought to ask her for it, but I just can't.

PRACTITIONER: What do you imagine would happen, if you asked her to repay you? [*hypothetical question*]

CLIENT: Oh! I don't know really. I haven't thought about that. I suppose she might get upset.

PRACTITIONER: And then what would happen? [*hypothetical question*]

CLIENT: She would get angry, tell me that I'm pressurising her and that will be the end of the friendship!

The client begins to identify what she fears and continues to explore how likely it is that her friend will reject her and what that would mean to her. She also talks about her difficulty in coping with anger from people that she is close to.

Hypothetical questions are also valuable for helping clients to visualise positive outcomes and to imagine acting differently. The following provide some examples of hypothetical questions.

• To a client who is expressing anxiety about refusing requests, you might ask:

'What do you imagine would happen, if you said "No" to her?'

or

'What do you imagine is the worst thing that could happen, if you said "No" to her?'

• To a client who is very anxious about giving a presentation you might say something like:

'If you were presenting confidently, what would you be doing?'

or

'If you were controlling your anxiety, what would you be doing?'

• To a client who seems stuck and says 'I don't know', you might say something like:

'If you imagined yourself "knowing", what would you say?'

or

'If you did know, what would you be doing?'

In the last example, the client is being asked to construct an imaginary picture. Exploring that picture may give him some insight into aspects of his concerns that he is overlooking, anxious about or avoiding. We will be returning to questions because they can be useful in assisting clients to gain different perspectives or to reassess their issues and concerns.

We continue with a word about *unhelpful questions* of which 'why', 'closed', 'multiple', 'either/or' and 'leading' are all examples.

'Why' questions

'Why' questions can be unhelpful to the extent that they put pressure on clients to justify or to find 'causes' or 'reasons'. Eliciting justifications may entrench the client in an existing position rather than help to see new possibilities. However gently asked, 'why' questions can also convey a hint of criticism. What may be heard is, 'How come you got yourself into these difficulties?' with the implication that it ought to have been possible to avoid them.

Clients certainly often do want to understand *why* they behave as they do, think the thoughts that they have, become depressed or have unsuccessful relationships. It is also one of the aims of using counselling skills to help clients gain greater self-understanding and insight into the ways in which they invite others to behave in certain ways towards them. Nevertheless, simply asking 'why' rarely enhances clients' understanding and ability to act differently. Exploring thoughts, values, beliefs, behaviour patterns and fears is likely to be more fruitful in helping clients to make sense of themselves, their relationships and their lives. You may notice that if you ask a 'why' question, your clients often respond as if you had asked either 'what' or 'how'.

Furthermore, some clients may not be interested in understanding 'why' or looking to their past for explanations. They may want to gain greater understanding of their current behaviour, and how that is dysfunctional for them. They may wish to increase their options, so that they do not repeat unhelpful patterns. Understanding 'why' does not of itself lead to action. What clients often lack is the knowledge and the skills required to act differently. They may need help in planning how to acquire them.

Closed questions

These invite clients to answer 'Yes' or 'No'. They are non-exploratory and can silence the most talkative client. Repeated use of closed questions leads to a kind of vicious circle. The client says less and less and, in order to obtain responses, the practitioner asks more and more closed questions. Consider the following example:

> PRACTITIONER: Have you told your wife that you have applied for this job?
> CLIENT: Well! [*pause*] No, not yet.
> PRACTITIONER: Are you going to?
> CLIENT: Yes, eventually.
> PRACTITIONER: Do you think she'll object?
> CLIENT: Yes, I do.
> PRACTITIONER: Is it difficult for you to talk to her?
> CLIENT: Yes, I suppose so.

This client faces a barrage of questions. He is neither encouraged to explore nor to expand on what he is saying. The practitioner ploughs on with what concerns her, following her own agenda. The session takes on a checking tone and the client may begin to feel harried or hopeful that, as a result of answering, a solution will be imminent. Now imagine the same session conducted using a mix of skills.

> PRACTITIONER: Have you told your wife that you have applied for the job?
>   [*closed question*]
> CLIENT: Well! [*pause*] No, not yet.
> PRACTITIONER: You sound hesitant about telling her. [*paraphrase*]
> CLIENT: Yes I am. In fact, I dread telling her. I think she'll be upset and not
>   want to move. There's a tiny bit of me that really hopes that I don't get it,
>   because of the upheaval it will cause. She has carved out a job and a life
>   for herself here which I haven't done, because I'm away from home so
>   much. Our social life has really been built by her.
> PRACTITIONER: You're torn, then, between wanting this opportunity and
>   wanting to keep things as they are for your wife. [*paraphrase*]
> CLIENT: [*slowly*] That's about it, I suppose.
> PRACTITIONER: I'm aware that your voice sounds very flat now. [*statement*]
> CLIENT: I feel really resentful and angry all of a sudden. It's like I'm saying how
>   dare she hold me back.
> PRACTITIONER: How dare she hold me back! [*restates phrase*]

In this second example, the practitioner uses restating, paraphrasing and statements. The interview is much more exploratory and the client is given the space to become aware of his feelings.

Finally, there are times when you may want to establish certain facts, to clarify a point about which you are unclear or to check information. For example, it would seem foolish to ask a client, 'How do you control your depressive tendencies?' if you wanted to establish, 'Are you taking any medication for your depression?'

Either/or questions

These are unhelpful variations of generally closed and sometimes leading questions. They are restrictive, because they present clients with two options when there may be more. You may also 'lead' clients, if the options offered for consideration come from your frame of reference and do not arise from thorough exploration. Consider this short example:

> PRACTITIONER: Will you tell her tomorrow or wait until she asks you?
> CLIENT: Neither, I don't think I'll tell her at all.

Multiple questions

This involves asking several questions in one intervention. Multiple questions are uneconomical because their effect is either to overwhelm or confuse. Clients may respond by answering one of the questions or by asking for clarification. In the following example, the practitioner uses multiple questions to respond to her client:

> CLIENT: I'm really concerned about my son. He's staying out late, being rude and offhand and telling me to mind my own business when I ask him where he's been. He's not doing his school work and I'm really worried that he'll drop out of school.
> PRACTITIONER: Have you talked to his teachers or his head teacher? Does he have a girlfriend or do you think he might be taking drugs?
> CLIENT: No. I don't think so.

The practitioner asked several closed questions. From the client's answer, it was impossible to tell which question she had addressed. The interaction was becoming muddled. The practitioner proceeds by checking:

> PRACTITIONER: Are you saying that you don't think he's got a girlfriend?

CLIENT: No. What I meant was that I don't think he's into anything sinister, like drugs!

The practitioner might have responded initially with a paraphrase and an open question, for example:

PRACTITIONER: You sound very worried about your son. What concerns you most?
CLIENT: I don't think he's into anything sinister like drugs. I suppose I'm worried that he'll leave school, because his exam results will be poor. Also, I'm sick of his boorishness. It's getting me down.

Leading questions

Leading questions communicate to clients, either overtly or covertly, that a certain answer is expected or that there are beliefs, values and feelings that they should hold or experience. Sometimes it is the practitioner's non-verbal clues that push the message, 'You shouldn't think or feel like this', or 'You shouldn't want that.'

Consider the following examples:

CLIENT: Sometimes I feel so angry and frustrated when he won't stop crying, that I could scream and shake him.
PRACTITIONER: Are you saying that you feel like harming your son?

The 'message' that the practitioner sends in her response will depend not only on her choice of words but for the most part on the accompanying non-verbal behaviour. Imagine yourself giving this response with a shocked expression and an incredulous voice tone; and then imagine giving it with a direct gaze, a level voice and a concerned tone. In the first instance, you are likely to convey that what the client has said is shocking, unacceptable and that she should not be feeling this way. You are likely to close down the possibility of further discussion. In the second, you will appear open to the client's fears and feelings and be in a position to encourage her to explore them. We are not suggesting that you ignore potentially serious information from clients, but rather that you do not communicate what you think and feel by leading or insinuation. Let us look at another example:

CLIENT: I don't really know what I want to do after my next exams. That's the problem. I'm sick of studying and exams.

PRACTITIONER: Don't you think most people feel like that and end up realising how important further qualifications are?

Here the practitioner is both communicating her own beliefs and generalising. She is 'pushing the idea' that 'this is a passing phase and you shouldn't give up now'. Leading questions do exactly what their label suggests. They control by suggesting a particular direction and by restricting the exploration to what the practitioner deems appropriate.

How to ask questions

- Directly – avoid prevarication or excessive qualification.
- Concisely – be specific and brief.
- Clearly – say precisely what you mean.
- Share your purpose. For example, 'I'd like to be clear. What exactly did happen at work yesterday?'
- Paraphrase the client's response to check that you understand before asking another question.
- Link your question to what the client has said with a bridging statement. For example, 'You mentioned feeling very hurt. What exactly did you say to her?'

The effects of questions

Questions will have both positive and negative effects, some of which have been mentioned already. Generally, well-timed, clear and open questions will have several *positive effects*. They will:

1 *Help clients both to focus and to be specific.* For example:

CLIENT: My partner picks holes in everything I do. It gets on my nerves.

PRACTITIONER: You're angry, because everything you do seems wrong. [*paraphrase*]

CLIENT: Well! not everything.

PRACTITIONER: What does she usually criticise you for? [*open question*]

Here the practitioner asks an open question to encourage the client to be specific.

2   *Assist information-gathering.* In the previous example, the client was asked to specify what she was criticised for. She replies:

> CLIENT: Well! Usually she criticises me for being broke. I always pay her back, so I can't see what the problem is. My money just goes and I never seem to get to the point of saving any.

The practitioner (and client) will begin to have a clearer understanding of this particular aspect of the client's relationship.

3   *Open up an area with a client.* For example, to a client who says she feels depressed and worthless:

> PRACTITIONER: What do you say to yourself when you are depressed and sad?
> CLIENT: I tell myself that no one will understand me and I'll never feel any different to the way I feel now. Sometimes I tell myself there's no point in living.

Questions are neither wrong nor unhelpful in themselves. However, overuse of questions is likely to produce *negative effects.* They are likely to:

1   *Increase practitioner control.* Even asking open questions does not necessarily mean that you will 'track' the client. You might still be following your agenda, as the following example illustrates:

> CLIENT: My partner picks holes in everything I do.
> PRACTITIONER: How long have you been together?
> CLIENT: For about two years and I wonder how much more I can take.
> PRACTITIONER: What first attracted you to him?
> CLIENT: Well I don't know. When I first met him I didn't like him very much. I wish I'd trusted that feeling.

Questioning in this way can invite the client to be a passive recipient rather than actively engaged in the process. There may also be an expectation that the practitioner will provide an answer or solution if the client is unable to do so.

2   *'Skew' the exploration.* Overuse of questions can lead to a session becoming a question-and-answer session in which little mutual

understanding is developed. Clients may have neither the opportunity nor the encouragement to say what is important to them. They may be indifferent, as they answer questions that may not seem relevant to them or relieved that the questions are not touching areas they are reluctant to confront. In situations such as this, the practitioner may become preoccupied with what to ask, instead of listening and attending to the client.

Finally, a useful guideline for probing with questions is to consider how the information elicited will help the client. For example, how helpful will it be for a client to acknowledge that she has hated her job for the past four years or that she and her partner fight about sex or that she is ashamed of how little she earns? Just as your purpose in asking questions in a selection interview is to gain relevant information upon which to make a selection decision, so your purpose in questioning in counselling is to make available to clients the kind of information that will help them to take charge of and manage their concerns.

Responding to clients' questions

Sometimes, as a way of introducing issues or as a defence against exploration, clients will ask questions of you. They may also want information from you. For example, a potential client who has not previously been involved in the type of help you offer may ask you what to expect. You will need first to 'tune in' to what the covert or hidden massage in the question might be and ensure that your response encourages further exploration. You need also to be aware that it can take courage to ask questions and be sensitive to the anxiety which clients may be experiencing. Therefore, it is important that you respect these questions. They often provide access to the real concerns of clients. Below are three such questions and some possible meanings and options for responding.

Question 1 'Do you think I'm crazy?'

Based on your understanding of the client, your experience of the client's concerns and the manner in which the question was asked, you may hypothesise that the client is thinking:

–   'Counselling is only for crazy people.'

- 'My mother is a depressive and I think I might be too.'
- 'I feel out of control. I don't understand my moods.'

No doubt you will be able to add more.

Here are some possible options for responding:

- 'You sound worried that you might be. Will you say some more about that?' [*paraphrase plus a question which invites further exploration*]
- 'I think you are unhappy and confused. I don't think you're crazy.' [*statement which gives feedback to client*]
- 'What are you doing or thinking that you would call crazy?' [*open question*].

Question 2 'What do you think I ought to do now?'

Options for responding include:

- 'What would you like to do?' [*open question*]
- 'I think that's our purpose here, discovering what you might do.' [*statement*]
- 'What do you imagine yourself doing?' [*open question*].

Question 3 [*Client talking about her relationship*] 'Do you think I'm being too demanding, wanting him to make a commitment?'

Some possible options for responding include:

- 'It sounds as if you think that you might be being pushy, is that it?' [*paraphrase plus a question*]
- 'I'm not sure what sort of commitment you want from him.' [*statement*]
- 'What do you want from this relationship?' [*open question*]
- 'You and your partner seem to want different things at present' [*paraphrase*].

Questions do not have to be answered directly or immediately. We are not implying that you should avoid either giving information or telling clients what you think. However, in the early stages of counselling help, when they are often at their most vulnerable, clients may invest you with 'expert power' and want advice or even to be told what to do. You will need to acknowledge their questions in such a way that you avoid either implying a course of action or imposing your views. You will be concerned to maintain the relationship as an effective helping relationship. How you respond will, of course, depend on the following:

- the answer you think the client wants
- what has gone on before the session
- what you think is behind the question
- the information you think the client needs
- what you consider a therapeutic response to be
- how vulnerable or robust you consider the client to be
- whether the client is coping with a crisis in their lives.

Making statements

Statements are gentler forms of probes than questions. They are useful alternatives for the occasions when you think questions might be seen as intrusive or inquisitorial. For example, instead of asking, 'What does your partner think of the idea?', you might more tentatively say, 'I wonder what your partner thinks of your idea.'

Like questions, statements are valuable for gaining information, for shifting the focus and for helping clients to be specific. Furthermore, as when questioning, you may usefully preface any statements you make by a linking paraphrase or summary to acknowledge what clients have said. The following examples show how you might use statements to invite changes of direction in sessions. In each case the practitioner summarises briefly and invites the client to continue by using a statement. Remember, the primary purpose of exploration is to enable clients to talk concretely about their own thoughts, feelings and behaviours.

Moving the focus from others to self

The client has been talking at some length about her relationship with her husband and his treatment of her and their children:

PRACTITIONER: You have talked a great deal about your husband's behaviour towards you and your children. I have a clear picture of what he says and does. *I wonder how you respond to him.*

Moving from vague to concrete

The client has been talking about an impending reorganisation at work:

> PRACTITIONER: You've talked about issues at work and mentioned various people involved. *I wonder specifically what those issues are.*

Moving from diffuse to focused

The client has been discussing her relationship and hinting several times at money worries:

> PRACTITIONER: We've talked about your wanting to improve your relationship and raised several aspects. You've touched on the issue of money several times and *I wonder if money is a concern for you.*

Moving from content to feelings

This client has been talking about not getting a promotion she wanted. She is showing little emotion:

> PRACTITIONER: You have said on several occasions how much you wanted this promotion. *I imagine you have some feelings about not getting it that we haven't explored.*

Statements enable you to direct the exploration with a lighter touch than questioning. This is particularly valuable when you are moving to areas about which you consider clients may be resistant or defensive.

Skills Sequence for Exploration

The skills that have been discussed in this chapter are the foundation skills upon which the beginning and subsequent aims and strategies depend. In order to proceed, you will need to master the basic skills of active listening, reflecting, paraphrasing, questioning and making statements. These skills may then be used in different combinations and sequences, both to respond to clients and to enable the work to move forward. The strategies set out in the next chapters all require virtuosity in these fundamental skills. It is important that you are able to use the full range of foundation skills. It is not sufficient to be skilled in one and avoid developing your expertise in others. For example, if you are adept at asking clear, open questions, you will need to expand your repertoire to include the reflective skills. You will then have the proficiency required to respond flexibly by choosing interventions that will both enable and engage your clients. Proficiency in these foundation skills will also increase your confidence in managing what can be a demanding process.

Being Concrete

The strategy of being concrete and specific is important to the whole counselling process. Here we want to discuss the skill component.

Being concrete has its foundations in 'actively listening' to clients' verbal and non-verbal communications, becoming aware of the level of specificity with which clients describe both themselves and events in their lives will put you in a position to help them to a more specific description.

Consider the following example. A client reported that in her family any feelings other than happiness or contentment were labelled 'odd feelings'. She would say 'I'm in an odd mood today' or 'I feel odd.' For this client to find significance and meaning in her feelings, she must first begin to identify what she does feel. In this example, talking concretely means helping her to distinguish and label her feelings. Helping clients towards greater clarity about themselves – their thoughts, feelings and behaviour – and the contexts of their concerns provides the cornerstone for constructive change.

The most direct ways of helping clients to talk concretely are by using the foundation skills either to request or to offer a *concrete example*. Let us look at some instances:

- A client has been talking about her lack of confidence and reports that a close friend told her that she 'puts herself down'.

    PRACTITIONER: **What would be an example of how you put yourself down?**
    [*open question to request a concrete example*]

- The practitioner might also offer a concrete example of issues that they have been discussing:

PRACTITIONER: Is telling yourself that you ask stupid questions an example of how you put yourself down? [*closed question which offers a concrete example*]

- The following example shows how a mix of skills might be used to help a client to be more specific. The client is talking about failing to get a new job.

    CLIENT: I suppose I was being unrealistic in hoping to get it.
    PRACTITIONER: Unrealistic. [*restates a word*]
    CLIENT: Yes – they wanted five years' experience and I only had three.
    PRACTITIONER: So when you applied, you thought your experience might be inadequate. [*paraphrase*]
    CLIENT: Yes, I did. But I have other things going for me that I thought might compensate.
    PRACTITIONER: What 'other things' did you have? [*open question*]
    CLIENT: Good qualifications. Better actually than the person who got it. My rise in the firm has been rapid. I've proved I can learn quickly and take responsibility.

The client is beginning to talk concretely about his thoughts and experiences. If we do not encourage concreteness, we do clients a disservice, because they are unlikely to explore in the explicit and focused way that is the necessary precursor to action and change.

Summary

This chapter has defined the foundation counselling skills of listening and responding, and considered their use in the help that you, as a practitioner, will be offering to your clients.

We have categorised the key responding skills as either reflective or probing.

- The *reflective skills* of *restating, paraphrasing* and *summarising* are important for communicating an understanding of client concerns from their perspective.
- The *probing skills* include *questioning* and *making statements* and are useful for gaining information and changing the focus in sessions.

These are the core skills upon which effectiveness in exploration, challenging and action planning depend.

In the next chapter, we turn our attention to the Beginning Stage of the process and discuss the strategies appropriate for work of that stage. We will also consider the integration of these key skills with the strategies.

4

THE BEGINNING STAGE
Exploration, Contracting and Assessment

The Beginning Stage

Aims (the intended outcomes)
To establish a working relationship
To clarify and define problems
To make an assessment
To negotiate a contract

Strategies
Exploration
Prioritising and focusing
Communicating core values
Being concrete

Skills
The foundation attending, listening and responding
skills as defined and discussed in Chapter 3.

In the first section of this chapter we discuss the aims and strategies appropriate to the beginning stage of using counselling skills. The second section is concerned with planning and managing the first session with a new client.

Aims

The four aims listed above characterise the work of the Beginning Stage. These aims provide a structure for focusing your work and for assessing both process and progress. They are stage specific – that is, they are more relevant to the beginning than to the subsequent stages of the helping process. If you do not adequately address these aims, it is unlikely that your counselling help will have a secure enough basis from which to move through to the other stages.

To establish a working relationship

Counselling and supporting others demands much more than organising a collection of skills and strategies and building them into stages (Bond, 1989). It is fundamentally a human activity, characterised by a particular type of relationship between practitioner and client. While this relationship has much in common with other relationships (for example, close friendships) it is the specific characteristics of counselling that distinguish this way of working from other helping activities. Much has been written, most influentially by Carl Rogers (1951, 1961), about the defining or 'core conditions' for developing the kind of intense personal connection necessary for therapeutic work to proceed. According to Rogers and subsequently other writers and practitioners, an effective counselling relationship will be characterised by three core qualities. While these conditions or qualities have been described in various ways, the common 'thread' is the significance and worth we ascribe to clients themselves, to their experiences and to our contact with them.

Let us look briefly first at these core characteristics – acceptance, understanding and genuineness – and then at some significant dimensions of the relationship required to use counselling skills effectively.

Acceptance

This is akin to what Rogers (1961) termed 'unconditional positive regard' and what Egan (2002) referred to as 'respect'. Essentially, acceptance means valuing others because they are human. Clients may experience a variety of emotions at the prospect of discussing what concerns them. For example, they may feel antagonistic, ashamed, fearful or embarrassed. Often they judge themselves harshly and anticipate criticism from others. We believe that clients who feel judged or blamed are unlikely to feel secure enough to begin exploring concerns and disclosing painful issues. However, in order to work effectively with clients, you will need to be continually hypothesising and making assessments. For example, you will be making judgements about process and deciding when to intervene and when to remain silent. You will also be evaluating the effectiveness of your interventions and making assessments about the issues that clients bring. But at the same time, it is vital that you aim for, and work to maintain, a relationship that is free of judgements about clients as worthy or unworthy individuals. None of us relishes failure, rejection or labels such as 'useless' or 'lazy'. While clients are often instrumental in creating some of their own pain, the strategies that they have adopted are probably the most creative ones they have for managing their lives as they experience them. Clients are doing the best they can and, therefore, deserve neither blame nor condemnation. In other words, 'judge the problem and not the person'.

To accept clients means appreciating and celebrating their differences as well as acknowledging their experiences as valid for them. Acceptance is neither a bland nor a resigned attitude that colludes with destructive behaviour and self-defeating beliefs. Rather it is a strong, potent quality that recognises the worth of others and believes in their ability to change. To behave in an accepting way does not preclude, for example, refusing to be bullied by clients or focusing on aspects of their actions that are proving unhelpful. Nor does it rule out discussion of the possible consequences associated with certain decisions. Rather it implies receiving and giving credence to what clients disclose to you; and distinguishing between clients themselves – valuable because they are human – and their behaviour.

Understanding

This means attempting to grasp as fully and accurately as possible the messages that clients are trying to convey by both their verbal and non-verbal behaviour. Defined by Rogers (1951) as 'empathic understanding', it involves striving to see clients' worlds from their perspective and to be open to their experiences. Because we are all separate, unique beings, it is impossible for us to understand our clients completely. No one can experience clients' lives as they experience them, because of the uniqueness of their experiences. However, empathic understanding offers vital acknowledgement, witness and recognition. It is our means of moving alongside our clients and of helping them to move from a position of alienation from both themselves and others to one of intimacy. Although understanding is communicated by our verbal and non-verbal behaviour, it demands much more than applying a set of techniques. Unless combined with genuineness and respect it will have a 'hollow' ring.

Genuineness

The quality of genuineness is often experienced as the most challenging for anyone using counselling skills. It demands a level of self-acceptance and self-awareness, because the focus is on how the practitioners' external and observable behaviour mirrors their internal worlds. Analogous to 'congruence' and 'sincerity', genuineness is how we are 'as people' in response to and in relationship with clients. The quality demands authenticity, openness and 'visibility'; in other words being 'real' and without hiding behind a professional role. Genuineness in our relationships with clients does not carry an imperative to voice all our feelings and thoughts about the way clients are behaving. Clients do sometimes act in ways that are irritating, frightening or boring. To be genuine in a helping relationship means receiving clients' behaviour and reflecting on the impact it is having on you, paying close attention to patterns and themes. Crucially, and this is one of the reasons why supervision is so helpful, it means separating what belongs to you and what belongs to clients (for an example see Chapter 7). Finally it involves sharing relevant aspects of your experience of clients with them, in ways that they can both accept and use (Mearns and Thorne, 1999). Your transparency and willingness to risk this kind of disclosure is a vital ingredient in promoting trust and safety. It also provides important modelling for clients.

Acceptance, understanding and genuineness are inextricably bound and we have separated them here for the purposes of discussion. They are the fundamental values that you will need to express, by both your verbal and non-verbal behaviour, in order to build the relationship as a working alliance. Clients may feel neither 'equal' nor 'powerful'. On the contrary, they may feel inept, powerless and 'one down'. However, a relationship in which they are respected, acknowledged and where they experience genuine interest in them together with a willingness to understand their perspective can be powerful in freeing them to become active in the helping process.

If the general aim of counselling help is to empower, then this needs to be reflected in the way you are and the manner in which you negotiate the relationship from the outset.

Other important and distinguishing aspects of the relationship may be conceptualised as follows.

Support/challenge

By support we mean being a source of strength to, standing alongside, and not colluding with or rescuing. While supporting clients is important throughout, it may be particularly crucial to the early stage when the relationship is fragile. However, if clients are to change, they will invariably need to face those aspects of their behaviour that are inhibiting change. Challenging clients means encouraging them to explore more deeply and to gain greater self-understanding. Challenges that are not based on support are likely to be experienced as dismissive or unfeeling. Support without challenge may be ineffectual because clients are never enabled to shift beyond their own limiting perspectives. However, if you are generous with your support, clients are likely to receive and use the challenges.

Trust/mistrust

Clients are more likely to sustain their work with you if they have confidence in you and experience you as trustworthy. They often seek counselling help because they have issues about trust: they may mistrust life, other people and ultimately themselves (Jacobs, 1998). Developing trust demands reliability and consistency in your behaviour towards clients, together with working ethically and responsibly. The basis of helping clients to develop resilience and to negotiate change is the constancy you provide in maintaining both personal and professional boundaries, for example confidentiality and timekeeping. The core qualities will provide you with some important anchors when both you and your relationships with your clients are tested. Building a climate where clients experience acceptance and understanding when they are dismissing, attacking and hating either you or themselves provides safety and containment. Clients need to trust that you can stay the course with them and to know that you are not going to buckle under the weight of their feelings and disclosures.

Limited reciprocity

While the relationship involves a growing mutual understanding, the sharing you will do with clients will inevitably have limits. You may decide to discuss aspects of your own life and experiences; the purpose of your disclosure will be to encourage your clients' exploration and insight.

However sympathetic you feel towards clients or warmed by their interest in you, the focus should remain on them and their issues. Our experience is that clients are usually content with a direct answer to a personal question, rarely wanting to pursue it further. Some clients may consciously or otherwise want to exceed the boundaries you are striving to preserve. There are many reasons why they might want to do this. For example, they may find disclosure so painful that they resist by attempting to engage you in gossip; or feel so unlovable and lonely that enticing you into a friendship will serve to confirm their worth. These are difficult issues to handle well and some options for managing these situations sensitively will be outlined in Chapter 5.

Emotional closeness/emotional distance

Clients will both tolerate and need varying degrees of emotional closeness with you. The practitioner's role carries the tension of knowing clients' innermost thoughts and feelings, being emotionally close to them and yet remaining distant enough to retain a helpful and 'objective' stance. You will endeavour to make emotional connection while remaining at an emotional distance; achieving that balance will enable you to avoid becoming both personally involved and overwhelmed, or aloof. Some clients may want the relationship to develop and to become romantically or sexually involved with you. This is understandable – receiving attention, unconditional respect and validation are powerful experiences, particularly for clients who have lacked these in their relationships with others. The tension in 'closeness at a distance' is an important ingredient in protecting the relationship as a 'helping relationship' and one that is consistent with the ethical boundaries of the practitioner's role.

Finally, while your aim at the outset will be to create a working relationship, attending to the relationship will be a continuing and important task extending throughout your period of contact with the client. As your work progresses your relationships with clients will change. They may have unsteady beginnings or go through periods of confusion and turmoil before they emerge strong enough to allow free and open dialogue. Your relationship with clients is one of the most valuable sources of information that you will both have. Clients will show you much – by the manner in which they relate to you – about the 'shape' and 'patterns' of other relationships in their lives. However, the initial stage of working together may be likened to laying down secure building foundations. The working relationship needs a firm ethical basis upon which to stand and from which to develop.

To clarify and define problems

This is evidently an important aim not simply for the Beginning Stage but throughout the whole process. The rationale of this model is problem resolution and taking control of problematic concerns. However unclear or however precise your clients are at the outset, you will need to clarify what issues and concerns you are going to address. You will want to establish as concretely as possible how they view themselves and their problems; for example, what they believe and feel as well as what they experience, in addition to understanding the relationships with whoever else is involved and affected. Clients will vary in the amount of help they need to do this. They may be vague and confused, and open with the following kind of statement:

> CLIENT: I don't understand it, I'm not bad looking and I've a good job and money. I want a relationship and yet all the women I fancy, don't fancy me. What's wrong with me?

They may also express their problems as 'feelings', the meaning and significance of which they do not understand, for example:

> CLIENT: I feel awful and I don't know what's wrong with me. I shouldn't be so depressed; I've got nothing to be miserable about, yet I am. I keep crying for no reason.

Equally, some clients will have previously thought through what the issues are for them and be clear about what they want to achieve, as in the following example:

> CLIENT: It's my job! I hate it, it's boring, and I need a change. I can't stand the people; they're all so 'phoney'. The problem is, though, the work is really well paid and I'm used to having plenty of money. So I feel trapped. When I think of leaving, I feel relieved and then scared. I want to go but I'm frightened of being 'broke' – so I go round in a circle! I need some help to think all the issues through.'

Finally, the fact that clients present their problems in a precise manner should not deter you from seeking further clarification. It may be very tempting to move straight to action with a client who says something like:

CLIENT: Basically, I'm stressed out and I need some stress management techniques. I don't go in for all this meditation stuff either, just to warn you.

This is not to imply that you ignore clients' views or wants but rather that you provide the time to explore their opening statements. In the previous example, you might want to acknowledge the client's assessment, reassure that there are other techniques for managing stress that do not involve meditation and then ask them to tell you how they experience being 'stressed out'.

Clarifying and defining, of course, continue throughout your work together and are not linear activities. Clients' views of themselves or of others and of their problems often change as the work progresses and they gain new insights. Rather prosaically, this aspect of the process seems to us analogous to emptying a washing machine. The clothes come out in a tangled heap and the first task is to separate and sort them. So clients and their concerns are often snarled up and confused. You will need to be able to tolerate this confusion and help them towards greater clarity. This means neither seeking to package clients' concerns neatly nor assuming responsibility for defining the issues for them when frustration or anxiety builds. It requires, instead, embracing uncertainty, staying with complexity and ambiguity, being open to new information and avoiding premature actions and conclusions based on minimal exploration. Clarifying and reaching a common, working understanding with clients is an important activity, begun at the outset and forming the basis for subsequent deeper exploration, goal setting and action.

To clarify and define in the Beginning Stage means that both you and your clients are working towards a common 'good enough' understanding of what the issues and concerns are for them. It also means that you have started to acquire enough relevant information about how clients see themselves and their concerns in order to make an assessment and to facilitate contracting.

To make an assessment

Assessment is an integral part of the counselling process and of using counselling skills. It has several important aspects. Your training and your role will necessarily orientate you towards particular theoretical frameworks for both identifying and assessing the nature of client problems together with the context in which these problems occur.

Your theoretical stance will also determine how you gauge what might be done to resolve clients concerns. That may include deciding whether counselling or some other intervention would be appropriate. During the preliminary assessment and any subsequent diagnoses, it is important not to lose sight of the core conditions and to remember that assessment is a continuous process. Any decisions you make or hypotheses that you formulate need to be kept under review. Supervision will help you to keep an 'open' perspective and re-evaluate your judgements. None of us is without bias and, in fact, the very theoretical positions we espouse predispose us to think about problems and resolutions in a particular manner. There are competing perspectives on assessment and diagnosis in the counselling and therapeutic world and it is not within the scope of this book either to address them or to discuss the wide variety of approaches and techniques available to counsellors. You may want to consult *Client Assessment* edited by Palmer and McMahon (1997) for a valuable introduction to assessment issues, procedures and practice. The other books in the 'Counselling in Action' series are also helpful references.

However, we want to mention one framework that addresses the content of what clients bring. Gilmore (1973) proposes a broad classification that identifies three dimensions to our existence. These dimensions are work, relationships and identity. At each developmental stage in our lives, each of the dimensions presents us with particular developmental tasks:

1   *Work.* This refers to what we are *doing* with the time, energy and resources at our disposal. At every stage in life each one of us faces the task of how to invest our energy to make life safer, more enjoyable and more satisfying. This dimension encompasses more than work as employment and includes all of the many activities, goals and the ambitions that each of us pursues.
2   *Relationships.* This dimension embraces the complexities of the relationships upon which we depend both for our existence and our

sustenance. Relationships are not static; they either grow and develop or become distant and wither. We all *move* in relation to each other in order to give and to receive care (physical and emotional), support, encouragement, stability and continuity. In considering the salient relationship issues for your clients, you will be asking the question: 'Whom do they support and who provides support for them?'

3   *Identity*. While each one of us has much in common with others, we must all cope with our separateness and our uniqueness as well as our sense of inter-relatedness and connectedness to others. We ultimately are responsible for deciding what is important and what is unimportant to us, for discovering how we make choices, for identifying options and for responding to demands made upon us. None of us can 'delegate' our existence; each one of us is responsible for choosing who we are and how we want to act.

This framework does not imply that clients' lives can be or should be compartmentalised. Rather it provides a way both of identifying the strands that are present in all our lives and of finding a focus for the work. It will enable you to answer the questions 'In what way is it useful to the client to discuss what we are discussing now?' and 'Are there other issues on which the client might usefully focus?' It is also a very accessible framework; clients can very quickly use it to think about how and where they invest their energy and time.

An initial assessment, possibly taking more than one session, will usefully include the following questions:

- Why now? What has prompted this client to seek help at this particular juncture?
- What does this client want by seeking help from me?
- What has changed for this client either recently or since the initial contact?
- How does this client define and describe the problem; in terms of duration and persistence, trigger and causal factors, and effects on self and others?
- What has this client tried to do to resolve their problems? If the client has previously used counselling and other similar interventions, what were their experiences and the outcomes?
- Is this client likely to be able to make use of counselling or would some other help be appropriate – for example, referral to another agency?

- What mode of counselling help might be appropriate, for example individual, group, couple or family therapy?
- Are there any indications that this client would prefer a particular style? Would, for example, a more active, interventionist approach suit both the client and the presenting problem?
- What support systems does this client have? What constraints and resources?
- Am I able to build a 'working relationship' with this client?
- Am I competent to begin working with the issues brought by this client?

You will also need to be alert to signs of emotional and physical distress that would point to a psychiatric or medical assessment (Daines et al., 1997; Palmer and McMahon, 1997).

Proceeding with the Beginning Stage will involve other questions, for example about both the content of clients' problems and the process. Some questions to guide you are:

- What do I know about how the client invests his time and energy (*work*), the support and challenge he gets from and gives to others (*relationships*) and how he sees himself (*identity*)?
- Is the client talking about what she wants to talk about?
- What issues do I think the client is avoiding, or seeing as less important, or overlooking?
- What patterns or themes are emerging?
- What do I know about how this client thinks, feels and behaves in relation to the problems she brings? What action has she taken so far?
- What incongruities can I discern in the client's behaviour? Does she, for example, look and sound angry and yet say quite clearly that she is not?
- What is 'fact' or 'observable data' – that is, what does the client actually say and do here, and what hypotheses can I generate to explain these data?
- What does the client believe about herself, others and life?
- What do I feel and think about this client and the issues we discuss?
- How are we relating to each other?

The final two questions are especially useful and important. Paying close and candid attention to the impact clients have on you will invariably provide you with valuable insight into their external and internal worlds as well as fostering understanding and genuineness.

Assessment is not and should not be viewed as a procedure that is 'done to' clients as passive recipients. It typically involves intensive and extensive exploration, during which clients will hear themselves describe themselves, their concerns and their lives, perhaps for the first time. Clients will be participants in this process, engaged to a greater or lesser extent, and may be affected and challenged by what you are discussing. Involving clients may be accomplished not only by using your skills and clinical experiences but also more concretely by encouraging them to develop self-assessment and self-monitoring techniques (Nelson-Jones, 2000). While assessment is intended to lead to working hypotheses and a plan for the way you work together, it is important that you preserve an 'objective' and flexible view, avoiding the 'de-humanisation' of classifying or labelling.

To negotiate a contract

Counselling is a contractual activity. Insights from the way contracts are used in a formal counselling setting are equally applicable to other forms of helping, for example, coaching and mentoring.

A contract is quite simply a negotiated agreement between you and clients. It has the following two aspects. The first aspect is the *agreement for the type of help you are offering*. This means being explicit and clear about what you are offering and avoiding confusion with other types of support or assistance, for example friendship, a sexual relationship, advice or practical action. Potential clients may have little direct experience of counselling and this aspect of a contract should entail clarifying what is likely to be involved for them should they decide to work with you. This part of the contract may be particularly significant for those using coun-selling skills as an accepted and recognised part of their professional role, for example as a nurse, a tutor or human resources manager. The practi-tioner can be helped in determining the essential elements of a basic contract by, for example, consulting the relevant professional codes and ethical guidance.

Once you have an agreement for the type of help you are offering, the second strand of the contract defines the focus, content and direction of your work together. This aspect of the contract is concerned with what clients want to achieve and what you are prepared to offer to help them achieve it. This aspect of the contract is typically negotiated when outcomes have been sufficiently clarified. Agenda setting and ordering of priorities is typically a feature because clients often have multiple issues to deal with or problems with many facets.

Contracts are discussed in further detail later in this chapter. Suffice it to say here that they are important both for ethical practice and for managing the expectations that clients bring. They also provide us with criteria by which to assess what is happening as the work progresses and to decide when the work is completed.

Strategies

The strategies are:

1   exploration
2   prioritising and focusing
3   communicating core values
4   being concrete.

The four strategies above are indispensable to accomplishing the aims or intended outcomes of the Beginning Stage, which are to form a working relationship, to clarify clients' concerns, to begin to make assessments and to negotiate a contract. In other words, these strategies have clear and well-defined purposes. They are interdependent although we have separated them for the purposes of discussion.

Exploration

Exploration in counselling basically means enabling clients to examine themselves, their internal and external worlds and their concerns. You will be encouraging them, for example, to describe their problems and expectations, to examine their own behaviour, to clarify and find meaning in their feelings, to consider their resources and support systems and to consider how they might resolve their concerns. Exploration invariably entails helping clients in the often painful process of sharing their shame, humiliations, hopes and fantasies. In action, the process is complex and not without pitfalls. What we are asking clients to engage in is a process in which anxiety, distress, hope and relief often coalesce. As the practitioner, you will be responsible for facilitating exploration and will need both to reflect on and to monitor the process. There will, of course, be balances to be struck between:

- following what clients are saying and influencing the direction of the conversation
- encouraging them to open up on topics and focusing down on specifics
- allowing space for reflection and keeping conversation moving forward
- knowing when to go deeper and when to stay with the current level of discussion
- focusing on thinking and focusing on feelings
- moving between talking about past events and describing what is happening here and now
- talking about others and talking about self.

The following questions will help you to monitor the exploration.

How specific is this client being?

At the start, clients may be vague about what concerns them. For example, they may know they are feeling 'uncomfortable', but be unable to discriminate further; or they may have hunches that some of their behaviour is unhelpful, but be unclear as to precisely what it is they are doing. They may also use vague statements to protect themselves from the discomfort they anticipate they will experience when they describe in specific terms what their problems are.

For example, a client might begin by stating, 'Well, my partner and I don't see eye to eye any more and that's the problem', when what she wants to say is: 'Our sex life is grim. We don't have sex as often as I would like and when we do it's boring and predictable. I'm thinking of leaving him.'

An important aspect of exploration, therefore, will be to encourage clients to be specific about their thoughts, feelings and behaviours in relation to their concerns. Obviously, you will need to be sensitive to the clues they give and time your interventions appropriately. It would be persecutory to pick up each vague statement and attempt a full description – particularly if clients are hesitant or distressed. However, vagueness is unlikely to lead to clear, purposeful goals and action planning. Helping clients to become specific promotes both clarity and mutual understanding. It means avoiding interchanges like the following:

PRACTITIONER: How are you?
CLIENT: Well! Things haven't got any better.

PRACTITIONER: So, nothing has changed for you?
CLIENT: Not really, but things are starting to get me down.

A more concrete invitation might have produced more exploration and more information, for example:

PRACTITIONER: You look down, how are you feeling?
CLIENT: Well! Things haven't got any better.
PRACTITIONER: What's changed for you since we last met?
CLIENT: Well, things are starting to get me down more.
PRACTITIONER: What in particular is affecting you and getting you down?
CLIENT: Well, work really. The amount of work I'm expected to get through. It's been a nightmare. I don't see how I can stay in that job and work at that pressure.

In the second example, the interchange has more direction; the practitioner's interventions are more focused and the client is prompted to respond with further specific information.

Inviting clients to be specific and concrete puts pressure on them and exerts influence on exploration, facilitating both discovery and clarification. Being specific moves the process forward and helps you both to find a focus and a direction.

How focused is this client being?

In the early stage, the balance to be struck is between encouraging openness and amplification and concentrating down on key aspects. Clients are often confused, unable to understand their feelings and may shift from topic to topic, raising many unresolved issues and hitherto unexpressed resentments. This is neither unusual nor detrimental. Some clients may not have talked about their concerns before; some may never have had so much attention and space to talk about personal experience nor have felt so miserable. Others may seek to avoid exploring painful issues by frequent switches to different topics. You will need to help clients stay with and focus on the issues they have raised. We are talking about holding the balance between the necessary tasks of opening up and homing in. Your goal is to facilitate a direction for the work with minimal intrusion and imposition of your agenda.

Consider the following example – the client appears harassed and is talking very rapidly:

CLIENT: My life is so crowded. I just don't have time for myself. Everyone is on at me. Even my neighbour says I do too much; that I'm too ready to help. I feel like a pack-horse, loaded up and carrying others – family, friends. Even at work, people are always on at me – wanting me to listen or do something for them. I'm always the one who always has to pick up the pieces. Reliable old me!

PRACTITIONER: Sounds like you're overwhelmed and frustrated.

CLIENT: Yes, absolutely I am! I do cope though. My husband thinks I should change one of my part-time jobs. He says I could get more money somewhere else for less hassle. I think he's right, so that's a decision I need to make.

PRACTITIONER: So, you get by and you manage. You were talking a moment ago about feeling like a 'pack-horse'. I wonder if you've said all you want to say about that or whether you want to discuss changing your job?

Here the practitioner indicates to the client that she has changed her focus and reminds her about what she began by saying. Finding and keeping a focus is one way of introducing some structure into what is often a muddled and unpredictable process of discovery for clients.

How prepared are clients to talk about themselves?

We can review this aspect from the perspectives of *content* and *process*. In terms of content, it is not unusual for clients to want to talk about significant others, about what others think or have done or are doing to them. They may, for example, have experienced others as rejecting or hurtful. We are not suggesting that you adjudicate; but, if clients are to change the ways in which they act, think and feel, they will need to be clear about what they are doing and how that is unhelpful. They will need to distinguish what they can control from what they cannot; and take responsibility for themselves and their actions. This is not to deny that clients have legitimate grievances and very real constraints, such as lack of money, poor housing or lack of qualifications; or that the social/cultural/familial context to which a client belongs should be ignored. Clients do not live in a vacuum, and helping them to focus on themselves does not mean discounting the contexts in which they live and work.

You will also be interested in the *process* or *how* clients are talking about themselves. This means paying attention both to clients' verbal and non-verbal communication.

At the outset clients may convey a lack of personal involvement in their problems, understanding them as external to themselves. They may not recognise what they feel, or believe that the feelings they do have are somehow unacceptable As the exploration continues they may begin to describe their feelings but convey little ownership of them (Rogers, 1961; McLeod, 2003: 178).

To explore means helping clients to open up about *themselves* and their concerns in a specific and focused manner, so that they acknowledge their strengths and weaknesses, their achievements, values and interests. It also means taking stock with them of relationship resources and deficits, community back-up, together with economic and cultural factors. In summary, engaging clients in the exploration process means helping them to shift from a position where they describe themselves and their concerns in a distant manner to one where they 'connect' with their thoughts and feelings.

Prioritising and focusing

Clients often have complicated lives or multiple problems, as the following example illustrates. A client, a single woman in her early thirties, presented a concern about how she related to her parents and her sister. She talked about their unwillingness to see her as the adult woman she was and to acknowledge the changes she had made in her life. She had embarked on a professional training course and continued by discussing her impending examinations. She revealed that she felt overwhelmed by the workload and frequently panicked. In her panic, she described her mind as 'going blank'. She was frightened that she would be unable to control her fears and imagined that she would misread the questions and subsequently fail. She added that exam success was not only important to her career, but would enable her to relate to her parents as an adult. Her practitioner was aware of the interrelationship between the issues the client presented and how the impending exams might have heightened her awareness of her family relationships. However, in discussion they agreed to focus on exam preparation and techniques and to suspend work on her relationships both to herself and to her family until the exams were over.

It is not possible for clients to deal with every concern at once and they will often need to prioritise.

Checklist for assessing priorities

Which concern or aspect of the problem:

1   is most important to the client?
2   is causing most distress?
3   is most frequently experienced?
4   would, if tackled, lead to the greatest positive outcome?
5   requires immediate attention and which might be left?
6   could most easily be addressed or resolved by clients and subsequently give them a feeling of control and of success?
7   is appropriate for individual counselling help and which would be best dealt with in some other way?

Prioritising means agreeing with clients which of their concerns or aspects of their concern have precedence for them. Ordering priorities will provide an agenda and will structure the work. Whatever priorities are set needs to be kept under review. As clients explore, their views of what is important to them may change; they may also experience positive or unwelcome changes in their lives that necessitate some re-ordering.

Communicating core values

Earlier, we described how an effective use of counselling skills is characterised by the core values of acceptance, understanding and genuineness. The purpose of communicating these core values is to facilitate a transformative relationship that engages the clients in the process. It is not enough to expect clients to know that you accept and understand them. You will need to *demonstrate* and *communicate* these values both verbally (in what you say) and non-verbally (in how you say what you say), and how you orientate yourself towards them.

Being concrete

We have reviewed the skill component or *how* to encourage clients to move from being vague to specific. Being concrete is a significant strategy in the whole counselling process, because it is a means of making what is implicit become explicit, and of making what is elusive and misty more precise and transparent. It also helps to highlight ambiguities and uncertainty, because it encourages candour. Vagueness or lack of clarity affords neither an appropriate basis for increased self-understanding and awareness, nor subsequent goal setting and action.

Clients may often feel anxious when they are invited to be more specific about themselves. This is because vagueness offers some protection against both facing and dealing with problems. For example, it may be far less painful and shaming for a client to say, 'I don't think much of myself' than 'I'm too fat and unattractive and I believe other people think that too.' If you wanted to encourage this client to reassess her self-image and consider how to build her self-confidence, it seems reasonable that you should understand how she views herself now. Gaining a clear understanding of her current self-image involves helping her to take the risk of being explicit about what she thinks and believes.

Finally, being concrete inevitably means clients become more exposed to themselves and to you, because the 'mask' of vagueness is lowered. Your assessment of the level of trust and safety in your relationship will be your guide to how and when you invite a more concrete description.

In summary, these strategies are interdependent and equally significant. For example, exploration is likely to remain at a superficial level if clients do not feel accepted and understood. Without adequate exploration, prioritising may prove ineffective. The list of strategies is not a menu in the sense that you select some and avoid others. They are all important in achieving the aims of the Beginning Stage. Nonetheless, relative use may be made of them with different clients and in different sessions. For example, a client who has thought out clearly what the problem is may need less time exploring and more on prioritising. A returning client may have a legacy of trust in you and hence you may focus less on relationship building.

In the previous chapter, we discussed the skills essential for implementing these strategies and fulfilling the aims of the Beginning Stage. These foundation skills underpin every aspect of beginning the working relationship with the client.

The First Session

In this section, we discuss the first session with a new client and propose a framework to guide practice.

Hopes and expectations

Prior to your initial contact, in the minds of prospective clients you may have been given a form and a personality. They may imagine themselves in relationship with you and have fantasies about you as an individual. Clients also bring a plethora of hopes and expectations to the helping process (Oldfield, 1983; Mearns and Dryden, 1990). They may, for example, hope for a quick solution, some advice or the 'right' answer. They may believe that you are the only person who can help them or that no one can help them. Clients also experience feelings of relief and a renewal of hope and energy at the prospect of resolving their problems. Deciding to contact a specific practitioner or accept a referral is often the start of clients' taking control of and making an impact on their concerns.

It is important to acknowledge the place and strength of these expectations. Even the seemingly most successful and robust clients may harbour powerful beliefs about what may happen to them when they begin to reveal what they see as their failures. Your awareness of and alertness to your clients' hopes, expectations and fantasies will enable you to provide opportunities for your clients to articulate and explore them. They often provide valuable clues to understanding clients' internal worlds and how they might use the opportunity to work with you. For example, clients who report that they don't expect much may indeed have intractable problems. They may also, without being consciously aware of doing so, be signalling their ambivalence about the process. Contracting provides an opportunity for clients' covert expectations and fears to be made overt and available for exploration.

Nor are we as practitioners immune to pre-meeting expectations and anxieties. We imagine what clients will be like and how it will be to work with them. Our fantasies might begin with a voice on the telephone ('sounds angry'); or might be fuelled by remarks made on referral, for example, 'This is a really difficult case. I thought of you immediately because you'll be able to help him through!' or written in notes, for example, 'has suicidal thoughts'. You will need to be aware of your own fantasies and the pressures you place on yourself, as well as how you experience the expectations of others. Separating what belongs to you, that is your speculations and standards, from what belongs to the others will free you to connect honestly with clients and work with them to meet their needs for development and change. For a discussion of transference and counter-transference in counselling and other types of helping relationships see McLeod (2003).

Making contact

You may have contact with clients prior to your first face-to-face meeting. If you have the opportunity to talk over the telephone, you will be listening not only to what they say but to the ways in which they are speaking; for example, are they hesitant or tearful? It is an opportunity both to consider with clients what they want and to communicate to them that you are an empathic, accepting listener.

Checklist of questions to ask new clients prior to the first session

1   Who referred them and for what reason?
2   What issues or problems do they want to address?
3   Are they 'in crisis' – if so, what is the crisis?
4   Who else have they seen? If they have consulted a doctor or psychiatrist, you may want to gain permission to seek information.
5   If you cannot see them or it is inappropriate for you to work with them, would they like you to refer them on?
6   Is there anything they would like to check with you?

While you may establish the first session as an 'assessment' session, you may also want to encourage clients to use the time between your initial telephone conversation and first face-to-face meeting. It is an option to invite them to do some pre-session work (Dryden and Feltham, 1992; Elton-Wilson, 1996).

You may want to say something like the following:

> Will you give some thought to what you want to achieve? If it helps to write it down and bring the notes along with you, that's fine.

or

> Between now and when we meet, will you notice the times when you feel less stressed out and what was happening at those times.

These kinds of interventions encourage clients to become more aware of themselves and their behaviours, thoughts and feelings. They also help clients to concentrate on the positive, the times when they are managing or resolving the problem (Nelson-Jones, 2002).

Let us turn now to the first face-to-face meeting.

Introduction

It would be more accurate to talk of an introductory phase. Your tasks during this phase will be to enable the client to get started and to set the foundations for a working alliance. The following will help you to structure the opening phase:

1 *Acknowledge the client 'as a person'.* This means offering a considerate and cordial welcome, confirming names, roles and the appointment made. Some practitioners prefer to open this first meeting with 'problem-free talk', the aim of which is to engage with clients as people. A short discussion about aspects unconnected with their concerns, for example, the journey to meet with you, is a way of indicating to clients that they are more than their problems. Even a topic that is as routine as travelling will often give an indication of clients' resources, strengths or achievements.

2 *Acknowledge any previous contact or information.* For example:

   PRACTITIONER: I have some brief background notes of your meeting with . . . and I have read them. How have you been coping since then? [*statement and open question*]

   or

   PRACTITIONER: When we talked on the telephone, you told me that you were very concerned about . . . [*statement to prompt*]

3 *Establish a pattern* (Rowan, 1998). Clients may both expect and want you to take control for innumerable reasons. For example, they may believe that they are helpless; or they may be feeling raw and scared of revealing their pain. Your aim will be to enable them to explore their concerns in such a way that the pattern is established of clients doing most of the talking and sharing in the responsibility for the work. Telling, advising and asking too many questions are some of the ways in which you might either unwittingly invite compliance or collude with clients' helpless behaviour.

   The following introduction is likely to convey to the client that the session will be conducted on a 'question and answer' basis:

   PRACTITIONER: The doctor said he can't find anything physically wrong with you, is that right? You have anxiety attacks and can't sleep – tell me, what are these attacks like and when do they occur?

A practitioner seeking a more open introduction that offers clients a focus, together with an opportunity to start where they want, might say something like:

PRACTITIONER: My understanding is that your doctor suggested we discuss working together because you have been having anxiety attacks and difficulty in sleeping. Perhaps we could start with that.

In the last example, the practitioner began by sharing her perspective, using statements to prompt and to focus.

Some additional possible opening interventions are:

– 'I wonder what you were thinking about as you came here today?'
– 'Will you tell me what the problem is as you see it?'
– 'What did you you hope would happen here today?'
– 'What prompted your decision to get some help for yourself?'
– 'I imagine you have some thoughts and expectations. I wonder what they are?'
– 'What has changed for you since we spoke on the telephone?'

4 *Assure clients of your availability by confirming the session length*. For example, 'We have 50 minutes together now and we'll take some time towards the end of the session to review.'
5 *Give some information about how you work*. For example, whether you will take notes or want to tape sessions. Some practitioners and agencies prepare information sheets for clients. You may want to check whether clients have any questions about the information that they have received.

Let us turn now to some of the concerns a new client might express and how you might work with their expectations.

What is expected of them?

As acceptable and familiar as counselling has become, clients may still not know how or where to start. Reading and hearing about others' experiences is very different from being a client. It is generally unhelpful to say 'Start where you like . . .' or 'Start where you feel comfortable', because clients may neither like what they are doing nor feel comfortable.

To a client who says something like:

- 'I don't know where to start, perhaps you could ask me some questions?'

or

- 'What do you want to know about me?'

You might respond in any one of several ways, for example:

- 'What did you imagine you would tell me?' [*question*]
- 'What would be useful for me to know about you?' [*open question*]
- 'It's difficult for you to begin now that you're here.' [*paraphrase*]
- 'You said you wanted help with ... Perhaps you could begin with that?' (*summary plus a statement*)
- 'Tell me what concerns you most at present.' [*give a directive*]
- 'I will want to ask you some questions – at the moment I'm interested in what's troubling you.' [*statement*]

How you work

Clients, for a variety of reasons, may want to know what theories you espouse or what techniques and strategies you use. They may have clear ideas about what they want from you as a practitioner. For example, they may favour an active approach that focuses on what they can do now to resolve their problems and do not want to focus on their early past. They may also have genuinely held but misguided concerns about particular approaches or have previous experience of similar kinds of counselling and found it unhelpful. You will need to be able to describe how you work clearly, concisely and without recourse to jargon and be prepared to answer clients' questions openly. You might say something like:

> I'm interested in helping you to find ways of handling what is troubling you. I can best describe the way I work as listening carefully to what concerns you as well as to what you are already doing to cope. I think that by talking your concerns through in some depth and having the opportunity to stand back

from them, together we'll be able to find practical options for doing something positive about them. In order to help you achieve what you want, I may suggest that you check things out between our meetings; for example, keeping a diary or trying out specific options.

rather than . . .

Well, basically I have humanistic/existential orientations, although not totally so. I borrow from cognitive/behavioural approaches if need be – I work to empower clients, towards increasing their proactivity and intentionality. In the early stages, I'll be empathising with you and later on I'll confront any distortions I pick up. I'll be interested in facilitating goal-directed behaviour which enables you to achieve valued outcomes which in turn addresses your problems.

While the latter may be accurate, it does not convey what might happen in a session. It is confusing rather than clarifying. Jargon and technical language may be meaningless to potential clients and make you sound like a textbook. It also distances you from clients, and language that obscures can make already vulnerable clients feel even more intimidated.

Underpinning this model are certain values and beliefs that some clients may not be able to reconcile with their own attitudes. Problem-solving by working from exploration and reflection through reassessment to action is an approach that some may find incompatible. As a result of their life experiences, family or cultural backgrounds they may view neither exercising individual choice nor the importance of meeting their own needs as significant principles. Their reluctance to become involved in the process may be the outcome of having different notions of helping from your own. Be prepared to share and discuss various aspects of both the model and the process in addition to being explicit about the values that you espouse. It can be tempting to interpret clients' decisions to decline what you have to offer as resistance either to resolving an issue or to addressing a developmental need. Sometimes this may be the situation. However, these interpretations may also be a misuse of professional power to discredit clients who appear to be rejecting the kind of help that you are offering. There will be times when it is appropriate to support some clients in deciding to seek help elsewhere as an expression of personal commitment to taking responsibility for their own well-being. This also keeps the possibility of them returning to you, if things do not go as anticipated.

Will they be judged?

People often fear judgement from those they turn to for help. They may have powerful experiences of being judged and 'found wanting'. As a consequence, they may have learned to judge themselves harshly and expect and invite negative evaluation from others. This may be a significant aspect of the problems that they present. In the early stages, if you sense either their anxiety or an invitation to criticise them, you might want to reassure by saying something like:

> My aim is to help you to tackle what is distressing you and support you in making whatever changes you need to make to sort it out. I'm willing to work with you. You're not on trial here.

Here the practitioner affirms her commitment to working with the client and tentatively states that she will be inviting behaviour change. However, simply telling clients that you are not judging *them* is usually inadequate. You will need consistently to demonstrate your acceptance, understanding and genuineness both verbally and non-verbally throughout your work together.

We think it is both essential and respectful to address clients' concerns and expectations. The balance to be struck is between providing information, avoiding talking too much yourself and ensuring that the focus returns to clients. You will need to respond to their questions in such a way that they remain involved and encouraged. You may also want to state explicitly that any decisions made, goals set or action taken will be theirs; that you will be helping them and not deciding for them or acting on their behalf.

The following two short vignettes provide examples of opening phases. In both cases practitioner and client have introduced themselves.

Example 1

The client, Jenny, has been referred to a counsellor by a colleague who had no counselling spaces available. In her initial telephone call Jenny revealed that she and her partner had recently separated. She sounded very unhappy. She said that she had not consulted her doctor, was not on any medication and had not taken any time off from work.

PRACTITIONER: Do sit down, Jenny. [*Indicates a chair.*]

JENNY: Thank you. [*She looks down at her lap.*]

PRACTITIONER: [*waiting for a few moments to see if the client begins*] You said when we spoke on the telephone that you had recently 'separated from your partner and you were finding it hard to cope'. [*Practitioner tries to remember the client's words and opens with a statement.*]

JENNY: [*hesitantly*] Yes, that's right. Now I'm here it's difficult to know where to begin. It was such a dreadful shock when he announced he was going. I never thought I'd need counselling.

PRACTITIONER: It's hard to find a starting place when you've had such a blow.

JENNY: Yes that's right. I imagined it would be easy just sitting here and giving all the background, but it's not. I'm not usually so reticent. My life has been turned upside down. Nothing's the same any more and I feel terrible – in a kind of chaos – all jumbled up.

PRACTITIONER: You're in turmoil – coping with a shock. Tell me more about how you're feeling.

JENNY: [*angrily*] My life has fallen apart – that's how it feels. I get up, I go to work, I come home and go to bed. I feel dried up – aimless. I just wander about the house – I don't have any purpose. I can't concentrate on anything. He left three months ago and I feel I ought to have snapped out of it by now, but, if anything, I feel worse. I ask myself what went wrong. Sometimes I blame myself and at other times I blame him. One minute I feel OK and the next a wreck.

The practitioner's aim was to enable Jenny to begin. She listened both to what Jenny was saying and how she was saying it. Her priorities were to show both acceptance and understanding, and to set up a pattern where Jenny did most of the talking and did not rely on the practitioner to set the agenda.

Example 2

Phillip has sought help from his occupational health nurse. He has consulted his GP for help with frequent debilitating headaches coupled with high anxiety. The doctor had found nothing physically wrong with him. The nurse uses her training in counselling skills to inform how she responds to Phillip. She has had no prior contact with him other than a brief conversation in which he gave his consent for her to obtain background information from the GP. Both have introduced themselves.

> PRACTITIONER: Phillip, as I understand it, you've been feeling very anxious and experiencing frequent bad headaches. I have spoken to Dr A as we agreed and I understand that he has encouraged you to see me.
>
> PHILLIP: Yes, he told me I ought to see you. Apparently it's 'all in the mind'. [shrugging his shoulders, looking and sounding scornful]
>
> PRACTITIONER: You're feeling irritated because he's referred you on to me.
>
> PHILLIP: Yes, I know he wants to help; but it's like he's washed his hands of me. 'It's all in the mind' sounds so feeble and pathetic.
>
> PRACTITIONER: And so a part of you feels hurt because you've been written off for being weak.
>
> PHILLIP: Yes, I'm just too trivial for him.
>
> PRACTITIONER: Your concerns are too trivial. [The nurse makes the distinction between Phillip and his behaviour.]
>
> PHILLIP: Um! And I should be able to control myself. I've always been a worrier, but not to this extent. This anxiety . . . well sometimes it's more like panic . . . comes from nowhere and just hits me. I wonder if I'm going crazy. Do you think I am?
>
> PRACTITIONER: Dr A doesn't think so and I'd need more evidence than headaches and panic attacks. It sounds like when you panic you feel disorientated and that worries you a great deal. [The nurse answers Phillip's question and uses it encourage further exploration.]
>
> PHILLIP: Yes it does. I don't know what's happening to me. It's like I can't control myself. I go blank and can't think straight; I find it hard to breathe. I worry about whether I'll panic at work, in meetings. I can't afford to have sleepless nights. I've just got promotion and I want to be successful. I've done well so far and it's almost as if this anxiety will stop me – keep me down.

In this opening phase, the occupational health nurse acknowledges Phillip's hurt and irritation at the referral. She thinks that unless he feels free to express his resentment, it may inhibit him from collaborating fully with her. She also answers his question about 'going crazy' as honestly as she can.

Checklist for the introductory phase

This should involve:

1 *establishing a working 'pattern'* – the client talks and you listen. Keep your remarks as brief and specific as possible.
2 *responding to any questions* asked by the client as honestly and directly as possible.
3 *beginning to clarify expectations* of what is involved in the way you offer help.
4 *establishing the notion of shared responsibility* for working together.

Exploration

In the first session your aim will be to make possible a 'clear enough', mutual understanding of clients' concerns. While the emphasis may be primarily on clients' 'presenting' concerns, the discussion may deepen and include more profound problems. By 'presenting', we mean issues which are both uppermost in clients' minds and with which they sometimes 'test the water', assessing whether to chance discussing more risky issues. Presenting concerns are nonetheless real and often painful to talk about. Exploring them is rather like a 'dress rehearsal'. Sometimes clients will flag their core concern in their opening sentences. The message may be coded and they may move seamlessly on to other issues. However, remembering the clients' opening words and returning to them can often help to move the exploration forward, particularly if it lacks energy or becomes stuck.

We have used the phrase 'clear enough' to indicate that clarification is a continuous process, and not simply a one-off task. Clients may be confused about what concerns them and, even if they are clear, it may take some sessions before they trust enough to open up to you. Furthermore, as they begin to explore, they may see new depths to their difficulties or realise that the predicament on which they are focusing masks different and painful problems. Practitioners inevitably have to tolerate a level of confusion, uncertainty and 'not knowing'. This does not mean chaotic, unfocused talk, but rather working with the belief that the meaning is within the client and that there will be many possibilities and no single answer. The joint quest is to help clients to discover meaning and significance as a foundation for change.

You will also want to gain some understanding of the wider contexts in which clients' problems occur. By exploring the wider context, we mean inviting clients to focus on related aspects of their lives. A framework consisting of Work, Relationships and Identity may be useful at this juncture. For example, if a client tells you of her difficulties with work relationships, you may at some point ask her about relationships in other areas of her life. Shifting the focus from the presenting problem to exploring the wider context is not a licence to be nosey or mount a fact-gathering campaign. We all live in a social context and a problem in one area of a client's life may reverberate in others. The opposite may also be the case. Clients may cope very successfully in all areas of their lives but one – for example, the client who has a successful career, but a dismal record of close personal relationships. Exploring presenting concerns and locating these in the wider context of clients' lives will assist you in making a working assessment and negotiating a contract.

The following questions will help you to evaluate your exploration with clients:

- What concerns has the client focused on?
- What important areas have been omitted or not explored?
- What are the implications of these concerns for the client?
- Who else is involved? – When do these problems typically arise?
- What has the client tried to do about them?
- How has the client coped so far?
- What support does this client have?

Assessment

One of the assessment tasks that usually arises in the first session will typically involve making a judgement of how fitting it is for you to work with a client. There are several aspects to consider, the first being whether the type of help you offer is appropriate for assisting the client to achieve their goals. Some other intervention may be more apt. For example, counselling or life coaching may be expensive in terms of time and effort, as well as money. Befriending or mentoring, although often provided at no monetary charge to clients, are similarly time consuming and requiring of personal commitment. Furthermore, there may be issues in your own life that you think might intrude unproductively; or you may have no previous experience of working with a client who has brought a particular concern. If either of these situations occurs, you will need to ensure adequate support for yourself via supervision, counselling or consultations with an experienced colleague. You may also want to consider referral.

At this juncture, assessment will include formulating a provisional agenda or plan. This will require discussing priorities with clients and negotiating the focus for the immediate work. The balance to be struck here is between developing a workable broad aim and subsequently formulating some interim or sub-goals that help clients to move towards that aim.

The decision to work together, along with aspects of the provisional agenda and the broad aim for the work, will typically need to be further specified in a contract.

Making a contract

Counselling and many other ways of helping that use counselling skills have a core value of client empowerment. Contracts represent this value from the start because they allow you and your clients to negotiate the terms of your contact. A contract can be defined as a specific commitment from both practitioner and client to a clearly defined course of action that establishes any business relationships as well as the therapeutic agreement. Let us look at the salient points in that definition.

'A specific commitment'

This generally means that the following conditions are clearly agreed:

1 *Number of sessions.* Contracts typically specify the number of sessions together and the timing of any reviews of the work. Whether or not you do this will depend on the level of formality appropriate to the type of help you are offering, your theoretical position and clinical judgement. It may also be heavily influenced by agency practice, where the pressure on resources may mean that you are encouraged to confine your work with clients to a specified time limit. However, it can be reassuring for clients to have some idea of timescales. You might want to say something like, 'I suggest we meet for six sessions and then review. How does that seem to you?' Reviewing the contract also mirrors the practice of breaking down goals into smaller and more manageable sub-goals. If you are going to make a contract for a specific number of sessions, you will need to consider the number of sessions that will be adequate to allow both of you to settle into the work together with what might reasonably be achieved within that time frame.

Clients may also be ambivalent about seeking help, wanting both to feel better and to avoid the contact. This is sometimes behind clients' question, 'How long will this take?' You might reply by saying, 'I suggest that we agree on six sessions and then review, with the possibility of further sessions, if you want them. I'm not sure what you were expecting.' There seems to us to be nothing wrong in wanting efficient, focused work with a speedy relief from misery. However, this seems qualitatively different from wanting to short cut through a process. Another way of handling this question is to say something like, 'As long as it takes for you to . . . and not a session longer.'

2 *Frequency of sessions.* You will need to think about maintaining continuity and giving space for clients to process and reflect. The time between sessions is often as productive for clients as the time spent in them because, not least, they have the opportunity to review, to test ideas and to implement new behaviours.

3 *Timing.* Offering clients a regular appointment time establishes routine and can be an important factor in clients being able to contain their distress. However, commitments and pressures may mean that this is not always possible.

4 *Length of sessions.* The usual length of a session provided by counsellors is 50 minutes to an hour. This provides adequate time for some intensive work but not too long so that both of you become jaded and unable to concentrate.

In other types of helping relationships the contact time may be shorter. It is important in holding the boundaries that you are ready to start at the appointed time, even if clients are late.

5 *Payment.* If payment is required for your services, because you are working in an agency or in private counselling practice, you will need to state clearly what the fees are. Other issues might be whether fees are negotiable and when payment should be made, for example weekly or monthly. When discussing payment, you should also include any expectations of payment for cancelled sessions. For example, sessions cancelled with less than 48 hours' notice will be invoiced.

This part of the agreement is sometimes referred to as the 'business contract' because it specifies the terms on which you will work together. While these aspects are usually attended to in the first session, flexibility is important. For example, the changes in clients may call for changes in the frequency of sessions.

'A clearly defined course of action'

This refers to the results that clients want to achieve. As we previously stated, one of the purposes of exploration is to help clients decide what they want to change in their lives. This part of the contract may therefore take several sessions to negotiate, because at the outset clients are often unclear about their aims. They may be vague and tell you, for example, that they want to be happier, or less depressed, or less isolated. Your role is to help them to articulate their concerns with the intention of identifying clear outcomes that you can both work towards. You may find it helpful in this context to use *contrasting.*

Contrasting involves asking clients to imagine themselves behaving differently. Consider the following example. The client is talking about her shyness and lack of confidence. She says that she feels embarrassed at social occasions and is frightened of approaching people that she does not know. She reveals that at work she frequently says nothing in meetings, even though she may have a contribution. The practitioner asks her what she wants to achieve.

> CLIENT: I don't want to be so shy, I suppose.
> PRACTITIONER: How would you be behaving, if you weren't being shy?
>   [*requests a contrast*]
> CLIENT: I don't know. I haven't thought about it like that.
> PRACTITIONER: If you imagine yourself behaving differently either at a party or at work, what sort of picture do you have? [*prompts client to imagine a positive contrast*]
> CLIENT: Well! I'd be talking easily, feeling relaxed and at ease. I'd know what to say to get a conversation going.

The client is helped to imagine constructive alternatives to replace her current uncomfortable behaviour. If the aim is to help her to change, then both she and the practitioner must know what change she is aiming for. The contrasting behaviour the client describes is the beginning of identifying a clear direction for the work. Knowing what clients want to avoid or stop doing does not usually indicate what they will do instead.

Clients with unrealistic aims

Clients may sometimes raise aims that you think are unrealistic, not within your sphere of expertise or harmful. One option is to reformulate what the client has introduced and offer an exploratory contract. Consider the following examples:

> CLIENT: I'm really worried about my son. He's not working at school. I think he'll fail his exams. I really want some help on how I can make him see sense.
>
> PRACTITIONER: You do seem very concerned. I am very willing to explore your concerns with you and discuss some options for influencing your son. I'm not sure I can help you to make him work.

We can influence others' behaviour, but we have more control over our own. The client's aim in this instance is unrealistic. The practitioner responds by describing what she can provide and offers a positive reformulation of the client's aim. As a general guide, responding to clients' requests by stating what you can offer before you outline what you cannot or will not do, is encouraging and promotes optimism.

> CLIENT: I'll tell you straight, I'm only here because my boss suggested it. She thinks I'm stressed and need some help. Her constant bloody attention is stressful enough without me having to cope with these new work contracts and a daughter taking exams!
>
> PRACTITIONER: Well, we could discuss ways that you could get your boss off your back – if that would interest you – as well as looking at how you might cope with the other two issues you mentioned.

This client is reluctant and may also prove resistant to any help. Attempting to engage with clients who have been referred to you or clients who feel that they are 'being pushed into accepting help' is best accomplished by going with their resistance and offering them the possibility of a positive outcome. Saying something like, 'I can see that you don't want to be here. I would like to know what it is that you don't want' may help to open a discussion about what the client really wants.

Constraints on the potential contract

If you are practising within an agency setting, the agreement you reach with clients will have to take account of agency policies and practice. However, we believe that flexibility is important. Contracts are neither 'engraved in stone' nor something to keep clients 'in line'. A word about 'power' – whether we like it or not, clients often see us as ideal, powerful and expert. Some clients may need to invest you with power, while others might want to compete with you. You will need to be sensitive to that when making an agreement with them; do so in the spirit of negotiation rather than imposition.

Confidentiality

Finally, the contract should include confidentiality. Confidentiality is one of the 'basic conditions' of counselling and other types of helping based on talking and listening. Confidentiality is essential to enable someone to talk openly and freely about personally sensitive issues. The boundaries of confidentiality need to be stated clearly and where appropriate negotiated with clients. You will need to be alert to the clues (body language, hesitancy, facial expression) that may communicate clients desire for further discussion or information about this aspect. A clear general statement on confidentiality might be something like:

> What you say and do here is confidential. However, I want to say something to you that I say at the outset to every client. If I think you are in danger of harming yourself or anyone else, I may take steps to involve others. I will, if possible, discuss this with you first. Are there are any questions you want to ask me about that?

If you are practising in an agency setting, the limits to confidentiality may be clearly outlined in policy and practice guidelines. More specifically, a practitioner in such a setting might say something like:

> Before we start and you tell me anything about your concerns, I want to talk about confidentiality. It is our policy that we will keep confidential whatever our clients tell us in sessions. There are exceptions; these are concerning [specify]. Should you at any time tell me that either you or anyone known to you is involved in [specify], then I will not be able to hold that information confidential. I will discuss with you how we move to involve others and hopefully gain your commitment to do so.

(For further reading on issues of confidentiality in counselling and related services see Bond (2000) and Jenkins (1997).)

To summarise: the contract is important in both the development and maintenance of the working relationship. It is a highly significant process whereby clients are offered enough safety, protected space, containment and freedom within clear limits. Contracts also help us to establish an appropriate position in clients' lives and provide a framework that contains the helping relationship.

Checklist for contracts

1   number of sessions – review
2   frequency of sessions
3   timing – when
4   length of session – in formal counselling typically 50 minutes to 1 hour
5   payment – when? how much?
6   confidentiality
7   goal of working together.

Closure

Let us look briefly at how you might end the first session by identifying some of the purposes of an ending phase. They include to:

- Begin to give clients a positive experience of ending. Some may have a history of being and/or feeling dumped. They may fear that what they have revealed is so unpleasant that you will not possibly want to go on working with them.
- Confirm your commitment to clients. Again some are anxious and may feel unworthy of your attention and time. You may do this by summarising the main points of the contract and confirming the date and time of your next meeting.
- End on a positive note. This is not the same as placating or reassuring which is disrespectful. However, it may mean openly acknowledging the efforts which clients have made by saying something like, 'I have appreciated the way in which you have talked openly about painful concerns here today.'

Managing session endings is one way that you can provide structure and safety. You may want to do some or all of the following:

- Remind clients of the time available and signal the ending. It helps clients to feel less pressurised if you introduce this positively and explicitly. Covert glances at a clock do not signal open communication. For example, you might say, 'We're doing fine, we have 15 minutes left. Let's recap and take stock of where we've got to so far.'
- Summarise the main points of the session in order to check your understanding.
- Confirm subsequent sessions.
- Make a commitment to begin with a particular issue in the next session. This can be one way of reassuring clients who raise new and important material towards the end of a session. You might say, 'I think that seems too important to discuss in the five minutes we have left. We could pick that up next week.'
- Discuss and agree any interim tasks, for example, diary or record keeping.

The ending of the first session is a strategic moment in working together in which the practitioner's respect for the client and the possibility of purposeful progress can be affirmed. This is a temporary ending until the next session. Preparation for a more sustained or permanent ending is discussed in Chapter 6.

Checklist for the first session

1 Making contact
2 Introduction
3 Exploration – of presenting and related concerns
4 Assessment – begin to form a working assessment of clients and their concerns
5 Contract – what the client wants to achieve
6 Closing – how to end

5

THE MIDDLE STAGE
Reassessment and Challenging

The Middle Stage

Aims (the intended outcomes)
To reassess problems and concerns
To maintain the working relationship
To work to the contract

Strategies
Challenging by:
Confrontation
Giving feedback
Giving information
Giving directives
Self-disclosure or self-sharing
Immediacy
Communicating core values

Skills
The foundation skills outlined in Chapter 3 and used in various
combinations provide the basis for the above complex strategies.

This chapter discusses the aims, strategies and skill sequences appropriate for moving the counselling work beyond the initial stage of problem definition and assessment. We will also consider some of the difficulties that you may encounter during this stage, together with some options for addressing them.

The Middle Stage is concerned primarily with helping clients to see themselves and their concerns in a new and more empowering light. In the Beginning Stage of counselling, you will have been concerned to understand clients' problems from their own frames of reference. In this stage, you will be influencing them to modify their frames of reference and to adopt different views or perspectives. The main strategy that you will use to influence clients is called challenging. It is challenging that stimulates clients to review and to question their current beliefs, feelings and behaviours and embrace more liberating perspectives.

The work of this stage evolves and develops from the work done in the Beginning Stage. By now you will have gained a clearer understanding, not only of what concerns clients but also how they interpret their concerns; so you will be in a position to encourage the development of new insights. Furthermore, challenging is a powerful strategy which places demands on clients to risk facing aspects of themselves and their situations that they may be avoiding or overlooking. Effective challenges are based in trusting relationships in which clients experience being both accepted and understood.

In tandem with the strategies, we will be showing how the reflective and probing skills (see Chapter 3) can be used to challenge clients. Effective challenging requires great sensitivity in order to fulfil the aims of this stage. Let us turn now to a discussion of the three aims of the Middle Stage.

Aims

To reassess problems and concerns

We are using the term reassessment to mean helping clients to form more empowering and enabling views of themselves and their concerns. This process has been called 'reframing' by Watzlawick and others (1974), 'redefining' by Reddy (1987) and 'new perspectives' by Egan (2002). Reassessment or reframing is important because it enables the client to adopt a new position in relation to the problems or issues that are causing concern. This often releases a new sense of hope and energy that can contribute to overcoming any obstacles to change. Clients who are unable to reframe their problem or develop new insights are more likely to remain stuck with the disabling perspectives that may have prompted them to seek help. The intention is to stimulate a shift in clients' assessment of both the *meaning* and *significance* of their concerns, so that the possibilities for change begin to emerge. Reassessment moves clients towards the 'brink' of goals and action. It is often the point in counselling where clients withdraw energy from problems and start to invest in a resolution.

Reassessment does not involve either disputing or contesting concrete information. It is concerned with interpretation and illumination, as the following brief example illustrates. The client Barbara has recently had her fortieth birthday. She tells her counsellor that she feels miserable and depressed. Her voice is full of regret as she recounts how reaching 40 is a landmark for her. She wanted a permanent relationship and children. She believes that not having achieved these goals by the age of 40 means that she never will.

In this example, reassessment does not mean disputing either her age or her feelings. Nor does it mean placating or sympathising. In Barbara's case, it might well involve helping her to acknowledge her disappointments and mourn her losses before beginning to help her to shape a different and more revitalising view of what being 40 means. For example, being 40 does not mean that she will never find a partner with whom to share the rest of her life; many people do so well beyond this age. Neither does it mean that she cannot have a sexual relationship or that a life without a partner has to be sterile and emotionally barren. It is her view of what being 40 means that is imprisoning her, not the fact of her chronological age.

A metaphor that illustrates this complex and important process is the simple one of framing a print. Different borders and types of frames will enhance different aspects of the picture. Certain colours and hues will either become more prominent or appear more subdued. Some frames will do nothing to enhance the picture and render it drabber and less interesting to our eyes. In all of this the picture itself will not have changed; rather, different aspects of its colour and form will have been intensified and, consequently, we will perceive it differently

What makes reassessment so powerful is that once we have been faced with alternatives, it is less easy to return to our former view of reality. If we return to the picture metaphor, once we have seen a border and a frame that really suit the print, it is hard to envisage or accept it framed in a different way.

In order to help clients to reassess, you will need both to understand and to take their current views of reality into account. That is the work of the Beginning Stage. Clients do understand themselves and their concerns but they may understand them in ways that are often self-defeating, constricting and immobilising. For example:

- Pamela complains that she is unappreciated for whatever she does for her partner and family. As she talks, the practitioner forms the view that what Pamela sees as helping, her family may see as stifling and controlling.

- Jack sees himself as strong, sociable and 'always willing to debate'. He tries frequently to 'debate' with his practitioner who begins to experience Jack as domineering and argumentative. She realises that she feels verbally battered by him and guesses that his family and friends feel the same.
- Liz is a team leader. She sees herself as tough, no nonsense and direct. Her line manager, when he observes her interactions with others, sees her approach as 'bullying' and intimidating.

It can be painful for clients to acknowledge the extent to which they have been the architects of their own misery. It can take courage for them to face squarely what they may have been dimly aware of and yet resolutely over-looked. They need the security of a trustworthy relationship in which to take the risk of looking afresh. This is why we include the following two aims as being of equal importance for the Middle Stage of the work as for the Beginning.

To maintain the working relationship

When clients are encouraged to reassess, they invariably experience dis-comfort. Relinquishing their habitual ways of viewing themselves, their problems and their lives and facing the prospect of change may seem deeply frightening for them. Clients may have invested substantial emo-tional energy in maintaining their current perspectives, however self-destructive these may be. It may take time for them to understand or to accept another view as having any validity for them. The relationship that you have developed with clients will be the 'interpersonal power base' from which you influence them to reassess. By this, we mean that clients have experienced you in the helping relationship as an accepting, compe-tent, trustworthy practitioner, and as someone who is demonstrably 'for' them or 'on their side'. 'Being on the clients' side' means providing the safety of a containing relationship that allows for and accepts often painful or shameful disclosure without censure. It seems reasonable to suppose that clients will not listen to or use the perspectives of individuals whom they neither trust nor see as competent.

The process of reassessment inevitably involves exploration and reflec-tion at a deeper level than in the earlier stage. As a consequence, both of you may feel more vulnerable as well as more invigorated. Clients will be 'opening themselves up to you' in qualitatively different ways – approach-ing the edges of their awareness. You will be 'holding' their disclosures and your relationship will become expressively closer. This has rewards and responsibilities. Clients may well have sought counselling because they have been unable to sustain intimate relationships or have a history of abusive encounters. Their ways of managing closeness will become palpable. Maintaining the boundaries of this relationship as a counselling relationship is not only ethical but also vital to helping clients to express and to tolerate their discomfort, to feel free enough to question themselves and to look at what is risky.

To work to the contract

The Middle Stage, with its emphasis on the shift to deeper levels, may also be a time when contracts are reviewed and re-negotiated. However, any challenge should keep the contract in mind as a guide. In other words, you need to ask yourself the questions: 'Is what I am doing helping this client towards fulfilling our contract?' and 'At this stage of our work together, am I helping this client to understand his or her concerns in such a way that reveals possibilities for change?'

The aims of this stage prepare the ground for goals and action.

Let us now consider in some detail what challenging as a counselling strategy involves.

Strategies

We begin with a discussion of the process of challenging, and identify what aspects of clients' behaviour you might challenge. We then provide some guidelines for challenging before reviewing what we consider to be the main strategies for challenging.

The process of challenging

To challenge means to question, to create doubt, to stimulate and to arouse. Challenging in counselling refers to that group of strategies intended to motivate clients to reflect on and question their current frames of reference with the intention of adopting different, more empowering perspectives. Clients' appraisals of their situations are often potentially restricting; in other words, they may be using 'out of date' or faulty maps. The core aim of challenging is to enable clients to construct different and less obstructed views. It is from these different views that they will be able to identify possibilities for constructive change. The following example illustrates how challenging enables a client to reassess her concerns.

Margaret was a teacher recently appointed to a senior position in a large school. She was energetic and ambitious. However, her new job was going badly. More specifically, she was concerned about the poor working relationship she had formed with an older male colleague. He was a senior member of staff and one with whom she needed to work on close professional terms if her work in the school was to develop. She complained of his narrow-mindedness, obstructive behaviour and boorish manner towards her.

As she talked, it became clear to the practitioner that Margaret was a person who wanted change quickly and who might 'ride rough-shod' over those who stood in her way. She believed that her deteriorating relationship with a key colleague would not only reflect badly on her but also impede her.

During the first session, the counsellor listened carefully to Margaret's concerns. She appreciated Margaret's vivacity and striving for excellence but also experienced her enthusiasm as overwhelming and almost unrestrained. She was also aware that Margaret adopted a blaming tone and focused almost exclusively on her colleague's behaviour. The counsellor hypothesised that perhaps her colleague felt overwhelmed and patronised by Margaret. She also had a hunch that Margaret, in her keenness to implement her ideas, might come across as being dogmatic and insensitive.

In a subsequent session, Margaret continued with her concerns about work. She expressed her exasperation at her colleague's behaviour.

> MARGARET: He's absolutely unapproachable and rigid. He must have a *hide like a rhinoceros* to just ignore what's got to happen. Things have to change, they can't stay the same. Some of his ideas are so ancient. I feel so frustrated not being able to just get on with the job.

The counsellor thought her relationship with Margaret was sound enough to sustain a challenge. She decided to offer Margaret her perception of what she had been saying and to encourage her to focus on her behaviour.

> PRACTITIONER: [*tentatively*] I'm not sure whether this will make sense to you. From the short time we've talked together, I've come to see you as powerful and very determined; someone who wants to make an impact

in her work. I wonder whether your colleague sees your determination and desire for change as threatening. What do you think? [*challenges by offering another view*]

MARGARET: [*with surprise*] I'm not a threat. He's had far more experience than I have. Anyway, I'd be willing to work with him, if only he'd stop being so awkward and passively obstructive.

PRACTITIONER: You see him creating all kinds of difficulties for you and you aren't going to change until he does. [*challenges by pointing out the implications of what Margaret is saying*]

MARGARET: [*slowly*] Well, I don't know. I've always prided myself on being flexible. [*pauses*] I hadn't thought of myself as powerful or as a threat. What am I threatening him with? He's had so much more experience than I have?

PRACTITIONER: Any ideas?

MARGARET: Um! [*looking embarrassed*] I've been told that I'm a perfectionist, who doesn't suffer fools gladly. Perhaps, that's what I've done, dismissed him as a 'fool' rather than someone who is anxious about the changes. But I want to get on with the job and if I don't push, how will things change?

The practitioner's challenges enabled Margaret to begin to explore different views of herself as a powerful woman and of her behaviour as being 'pushy' rather than enthusiastic. She continued by considering the possibility that she had tried to effect too much change too quickly and been hasty in labelling others as obstructive. The practitioner was not concerned to referee or to blame but rather to enable Margaret to think differently about her own and her colleague's behaviour. Exploring a different perspective might help Margaret to reassess the situation and subsequently decide on an approach that would give her a better chance of getting what she wanted. In this example, the practitioner considered that Margaret had not 'owned' the 'pushy' and 'determined' aspects of her behaviour. In effect she was doing exactly what she was objecting to in her colleague's behaviour – of acting in a dogmatic and thick-skinned manner. Her final question provided the opening for the practitioner to raise the possibility of different ways of making change happen with her.

Challenging does not imply that there is a *right way* of looking at situations or that there is 'a reality' which the practitioner operates within and which the client must be helped to espouse. Rather your intention in challenging will be to facilitate the kind of deeper exploration that stimulates clients to reassess themselves and their concerns. Let us look briefly at what deeper exploration means.

Deeper exploration

Deeper exploration has a quality and an intensity which exploration in the Beginning Stage does not have. For clients, it carries the potential both for renewed energy as they gain clearer self-understanding and for discomfort as they begin to relinquish 'old' perspectives. At its core, deeper exploration implies a change in focus from the evident to the cloaked. The focus has turned to what clients are either unaware or dimly aware of, as well as what they may be avoiding, ignoring or overlooking. It has been usefully described as helping clients overcome 'blind spots' (Egan, 2002).

Deeper exploration evolves from the work of the Beginning Stage. This means that it is rooted firmly in a clear mutual understanding of how *clients* view their concerns, together with *your* appreciation of their concerns based on your different perspective.

In skill terms, it involves listening and attending to *what* and *how* clients are communicating, as well as to what they are implying, hinting at or omitting. It is listening for the *hidden*, the *unexpressed* or the 'ulterior' message, and understanding the possible significance of that for clients. Egan (2002) refers to this strategy as *advanced empathy*, meaning the ability to discern and understand 'covert' or deeper meaning. Essentially, as you communicate your deeper understanding of clients, so you will influence them to more profound exploration and greater self-understanding (Truax and Carkhuff, 1967).

It is hard to illustrate in writing a practitioner developing an understanding of the 'ulterior' and 'hidden' aspects, because much of the significant interaction is both subtle and non-verbal; for example, facial expression, voice tone, pace of speech, body posture or a fleeting glance. Accurately reflecting what your client is communicating relies on your ability both to sense and to distil the important 'kernel' from the packaging that may surround it. The following provide some ways in which you might facilitate deeper exploration:

1   *Focusing on what clients hint at or imply.* Consider the following example. The client, Josie, is discussing her dissatisfaction with work and says she is considering resigning.

JOSIE: I really can't see the situation improving. I may have trouble getting another job but I'm prepared to do temporary work until I find another permanent job that's suitable. I've been thinking how to answer questions at my 'exit interview' too.

PRACTITIONER: You said you were considering resigning – from what you say, it sounds like you've made the decision.

JOSIE: Yes, I suppose I have. I realised, hearing myself talk about temping and 'exit interviews', that I've stuck this job because I thought I *should* stick it out; that I haven't given it long enough and I *oughtn't* to leave quite so soon.

The practitioner encouraged deeper exploration by turning Josie's attention to what she had implied. The outcome was that Josie began to voice some of the 'rules' by which she lived her life and which had inhibited her from taking action.

2   *Identifying themes and patterns.* Themes and patterns can be likened to our 'default' positions or 'blueprints'. They are the habitual responses, feelings and thoughts that we fall back on irrespective of what the situation demands. Attending carefully to clients, you may discern patterns or themes which permeate their lives and which provide an explanation for what is going on for them now. Recognising and exploring underlying patterns helps them to gain some clarity, where perhaps previously they experienced bewilderment. Clients may give clues as to the patterns in their lives, for example, by saying something like, 'Here I go again' or 'This is always happening to me.' While patterns give us familiarity and a sense of control over our lives, some also stunt creativity and spontaneity. Clients may have patterns that are destructive to themselves and to others (Stewart and Joines, 1987; Stewart, 2000; Lister Ford, 2002).

Consider the following example. Janet is complaining of being 'used' by her friends. In an earlier session, she told the practitioner that she had looked after herself and her younger sister when they were both small because her mother had always worked outside the home.

JANET: I'm fed up with Ros. She phoned me again last night and never even asked how I was. She just went on and on about her problems. I listened and talked things through with her. But she didn't want to listen to me and hear about me. She said, 'It's different for you. You're so capable.' I suppose I am.

PRACTITIONER: You've told me how you looked after yourself and your sister. Now you are looking after friends seemingly more than you want to. I'm getting a picture of someone who has done a lot of caring for others in her life. Being a 'caretaker' seems to be a pattern for you, or am I reading too much into what you've said?

The practitioner identifies the theme or pattern of being a 'caretaker'. She uses a summary both to acknowledge what Janet has said and to offer her this perspective. She ends by asking Janet for her views. Janet goes on to explore the significance of that theme for herself and how she is attracted to people who 'need looking after'. In doing so, she begins to form a different understanding of herself and her relationships with others.

Although we have discussed challenging both what clients hint at or imply and the patterns and themes in their behaviour, almost anything that clients raise with you is amenable to challenging. We will briefly consider some further broad areas of client behaviour that you might usefully challenge.

What to challenge

Essentially, you will be focusing on the ways in which clients understand their worlds; that is, make sense of both their own and others' behaviour and the situations they are in. However, clients' understanding of their worlds is a very broad brush; more specifically, you might challenge when you notice any of the following.

1 *Making connections.* Clients may fail to make the connections that would enable them to gain a deeper understanding of themselves and their concerns. Making connections is rather like completing a jigsaw. The individual pieces have a meaning and significance when they are put together which they do not have when they are viewed separately.

  Consider the following example. During her first session, Nancy, a client, related that she felt exhausted, drained and irritable much of the time. She feared that she was depressed and, with some relief, quoted from a book about depression that she carried. Nancy was considering medication to help her 'to feel better'. After listening for a while the practitioner responded.

PRACTITIONER: You've told me something about your job and your family.
I'm not sure exactly what your daily routine actually involves for you.

NANCY: Oh that's easy enough. I'm in work by 7.00 a.m. so that I can make a
start before the others arrive and the meetings begin. I can also leave a
bit early, say 5 o'clock, to pick up the twins from the childminder. I
usually give them their tea and play with them until about 7 p.m. when
we start the bedtime routine. They're in bed by about 7.30 and then I
sometimes get our meal, if John is working late. We eat about 8.30.
That's about it, unless I have some work to do for an early meeting.

PRACTITIONER: From your description, I think your exhaustion and irritability
have more to do with the stress of coping with heavy demands than
depression. I wonder what you were thinking and feeling as you were
talking.

NANCY: [angrily] I was thinking 'How the hell do I manage it all!' I could feel
myself sinking as I was talking. It wasn't until I started to tell you what I
did, that I realised how crowded and fraught life is at present. Perhaps
you're right. I'm feeling irritable because I'm overtired and overworked.
I've also realised how 'ripped off' I feel, because I don't have any time
for myself.

This client was not making the connection between coping with heavy
work and family demands and her feeling exhausted and irritable. She
continued to explore how seeing herself as a depressed person was
preferable to 'being tired', because that signalled weakness; how angry
she was at not having time for herself and her belief that she had no
business complaining because she had chosen this life.

2   *Overlooking of resources and deficits.* Often clients do not have clear
and up-to-date pictures of their resources and deficits. As you listen to
clients, you may 'hear' how they overlook the skills they have or how
they dismiss what you hypothesise might be genuine constraints. If
clients are to begin to take control of their concerns, then being clear
about their resources and deficits, seems reasonable information to
consider.

Consider the following example: Carl is discussing a possible job
opportunity in a coaching session at work. The post seems just right for
him and yet he seems very reluctant to apply. As the coach listens, she
notices that Carl seems anxious and refers often to a previous job, in
another company, where he was under pressure from a bullying
manager and eventually made redundant. Although this was some time

ago, he now seems to view himself as a disappointment and someone who can't 'stand the pace'. Carl seems to be ignoring both his considerable success in his current job and the fact that he has been asked to consider applying for this post.

3 *Discrepancies.* As you listen and attend to clients you will become aware when things do not 'add up'. We will be discussing how to explore discrepancies in the later section on Confrontation.

4 *Lack of understanding of the consequences of behaviour.* Clients may be unaware of how their behaviour impacts on others. For example, consider the following exchange from a conversation between Joanne and the Human Resources Manager. Joanne is very frustrated and is accusing her boss of overlooking her.

> JOANNE: I never mind what I do – I do what is asked of me and I don't make a big deal out of things. I stand in for others, bail them out when they've made mistakes. Who gets the perks, the conference in Amsterdam – not me! I've never been selfish or hard-nosed like some people. I've always thought that if I worked hard and efficiently, I would get recognised.
>
> PRACTITIONER: You've been helpful and instead of being rewarded, you've been disregarded. I wonder if you've been too willing, too compliant and have signalled that you're OK with taking a back seat. Does that make any sense?

Joanne has overlooked the consequences of her behaviour. By not making her wants known, and putting herself forward, she has played her part in being overlooked.

5 *Beliefs and the inferences drawn from those beliefs.* Clients may have irrational (and unreasonable) beliefs that both inhibit and disturb them. Some of the typical self-defeating beliefs that you might discern are: 'I must be liked by everyone', or 'I must never give up on anything', or 'If I make a mistake, it means that I am totally useless (and therefore unlovable).'

Clients' behaviour towards you and their reports of their actions will give some pointers to what their belief systems might be. For example, the client who is apologetic, ultra-careful about his appearance yet frequently experiences your questions as critical of him, may well believe at some profound level that he has to 'get everything right and never make a mistake'.

The aim of challenging is to help clients to increased awareness of their beliefs; the inferences that they draw from them; and how their beliefs influence their behaviour. Beliefs are often expressed as 'shoulds', 'musts' and 'oughts', as if signifying an immutable rule rather than a choice; for example, 'I shouldn't be angry' or 'He should be punished for what he did.' An effective and non-intrusive way of beginning to explore is to use a reflection or one-word questions as in the following short example:

CLIENT: I can't ask him to help me – I've got to do it myself.
PRACTITIONER: Got to?
CLIENT: Because if I do, he'll think I'm lazy and incompetent.
PRACTITIONER: And then?
CLIENT: Well, I'll get a lousy appraisal and it will be curtains for my chances of promotion here.

Clients' belief systems are the guiding principles by which they live – they provide for regularity as well as protection from threats in the form of censure, abandonment, shame and deprivation. Helping clients to appreciate these guidelines and the purposes they have served for them is the start of helping them to become more relaxed, open and less rigid.

For a fuller exploration of ways of tackling erroneous and self-defeating beliefs in counselling, see *Cognitive Behavioural Counselling in Action* by Trower et al. (1988) and *Rational Emotive Behavioural Counselling in Action* by Dryden (1999) in the 'Counselling in Action' series. In his book *Effective Thinking Skills,* Nelson-Jones (1996) also provides some excellent examples of the oppressive beliefs which people allow to govern their lives, together with some useful interventions and training exercises.

6   *Unexpressed feelings.* Clients may find feelings difficult – difficult to experience, to make sense of, to own, to label and to express. They may act as though certain feelings are, at best, simply wrong or they may deny expressions of certain feelings such as joy. Sometimes too, clients will mask one feeling with another; for example, laughing to cover pain. Consider the following example that illustrates how awareness may be facilitated by helping a client to identify and express feelings.

The client, Bob, wanted to set boundaries on an ever-increasing demand for his time. He responded to any attempt by the practitioner to focus on his feelings by saying what he thought. The practitioner sensed Bob was angry and scared of acknowledging his anger for some reason.

PRACTITIONER: I guess you felt angry at being asked to work on your day off.

BOB: I don't think it's a matter of being 'put out'. It's my job.

PRACTITIONER: I notice that you don't say how you're feeling. Perhaps I've got it wrong and you don't have any feelings about losing your day off. Perhaps that's OK with you. [*Counsellor uses statements to give her perspective.*]

BOB: [*irritated*] Well! Of course I have feelings. When the phone rang yesterday, I told myself, 'Calm down. Blowing your top won't do any good.'

PRACTITIONER: And you felt?

BOB: Angry and 'hassled'.

The counsellor then prompted Bob to explore the significance of his anger. He realised that he often ignored how he felt and consequently complied with others' unreasonable demands. He also confronted his rigid beliefs, which were that he should never say 'no' and that showing anger was just 'bad'. The consequences of doing either would be rejection and isolation. Let us return to the notion of challenging to discover resources and deficits; Bob also recognised that he had limited ways of expressing anger (a *deficit*); he either withdrew or became unnecessarily aggressive. This became one of Bob's goals – to learn to express what he felt assertively.

Feelings don't exist in isolation; they are attached to something – past events, beliefs and transitions. They have resonance and meaning for clients, if they can allow their feelings to surface and guide the way. Challenging clients to explore their feelings gives them useful insight into themselves and their current situations.

Let us now consider how to challenge.

How to challenge

1   *Be tentative.* Challenging involves sharing your perspectives and hunches. Clients will be more likely to listen to and explore alternative views, if they are expressed tentatively. Telling or informing may seem dominating and is likely to create defence. It also puts the practitioner in the role of expert. Tentativeness does not mean diluting your

message or 'pussyfooting' with 'ifs' and 'buts'. Rather it means conveying that what you are about to say is open to exploration and modification. You might communicate tentativeness by saying, for example, 'I'm wondering if . . .', or 'How does this seem to you . . . ?', or 'My guess is . . .', or 'My hunch is . . .'

2 *Remember the aims of challenging.* People have become clients because they want to change their behaviour in order to handle aspects of their lives more successfully. In the course of the work, they may disclose aspects of their lives, about which you are tempted to encourage them to expand further. However, the aim of challenging is to help clients to reassess themselves and the concerns they bring, in order to effect some change. You will need to monitor whether your challenges are helping them to do that. Keeping the aims of challenging in mind is another way of keeping your work focused. Moreover, the decision about what to challenge should be based on the agreed contract and not on the practitioner's inquisitiveness.

3 *Consider whether the client is able to receive the challenge and use it.* Sometimes clients are raw and vulnerable. They need time to let themselves heal a little and regain their emotional balance before being able to face aspects of the issue they are struggling with, even though they are well aware that they will have to address it sooner or later. As a colleague once remarked 'If your skin is raw, even a small puff of breeze stings.' In these circumstances, the most skilled and insightful challenges are not going to further the counselling work, if clients are neither able to hear nor use them.

Clients who are in a highly charged emotional state may also not be amenable to challenging. Consider the following example.

A distressed pupil was complaining bitterly and furiously about what she considered to be unfair treatment by another teacher. The pastoral care teacher responded by saying, 'It does sound to me like you were being provocative – have you thought of that? Maybe arguing and answering back, even in a joke, just wasn't helpful.' On hearing this, the youngster stormed out in a rage. She was not willing to look at her behaviour because she was smarting from what she believed was unfair treatment. If the teacher had listened and acknowledged the pupil's point of view as valid for her and allowed her to express her anger, she might then have been open to considering another perspective.

4 *Keep the alternative perspective close to the client's.* Perspectives that are

too divergent may seem like wild guesses or invitations to engage in extravagant speculation. We like to think of a challenge as a 'glimpse of the obvious'. By that we mean that once clients hear your view, they wonder how they could have overlooked such an evident perspective that reveals important clues as to how they are behaving as they are. An example of a perspective that might be difficult for a client to use because it is far removed from what she is saying is:

CLIENT: I feel so lost now that both children have started university. The house seems really empty; I rattle around in it. I'm at a loose end and I'm shocked at how much I miss them.

PRACTITIONER: You mentioned that your father was away a lot during your early childhood. Perhaps your despondency is also to do with the abandonment you felt then.

5 *Be concrete.* Vague challenges are unhelpful because they do not express clearly which aspect of clients' thoughts, feelings or behaviour might usefully be explored further. You will need to state specifically and clearly what you notice or think. Consider the following examples.

A client presented as lacking in self-confidence and complained that he wasn't valued at work or at home. The practitioner noticed that he brushed aside any compliments or positive feedback from her. She challenged him in a vague and unhelpful way as follows:

PRACTITIONER: When I've complimented you or said anything positive to you, you've usually brushed it aside. I guess not accepting praise contributes to your low self-esteem. What do you think?

A more concrete challenge might have been something like:

PRACTITIONER: I noticed that when I complimented you on how you tackled your colleague, you said, 'Oh, that! Well! That was lucky – I just caught her on a good day!' You seemed to dismiss what I said. I wonder if you disregard or ignore positive comments from family and colleagues and then feel undervalued. What do you think?

Here the practitioner commented specifically on the client's behaviour before offering her own view. The intervention gave a much clearer indication of what the client might usefully explore further.

6   *Avoid blaming.* Effective challenging involves neither blaming nor finding fault. Clients are more likely to use challenges that are free of criticism. Helping clients to recognise and acknowledge unhelpful beliefs and behaviour, to 'own' and take responsibility for what is legitimately theirs to take, needs to be distinguished from condemnation and opprobrium. If you sense that clients experience your challenges as criticism, then you will need to address that openly. We will be discussing how you might do this when we consider the strategy of 'immediacy'.

7   *Encourage and facilitate self-challenge.* Consider the following example. A client, Penny, in her mid-thirties, was talking of a particularly harrowing break-up of her relationship. She focused on her partner's faults, and on the humiliations and hurt she had suffered. She presented herself as the 'good', reasonable partner, who was a victim in the whole painful affair. Penny was resistant to any invitations to explore the dynamics of the relationship. It was not until some weeks later when she said, in a quiet voice, 'I guess Rob and I were really bad for one another', that the practitioner realised that Penny had begun to challenge herself and to reassess her version of past events. She was shifting from a position of 'it's all his fault' to a view of 'perhaps I also contributed to what went wrong'. The way was then open for the counsellor to encourage Penny to explore how she allowed herself to be oppressed to the point where she became depressed and physically run down.

You can encourage *self-challenge* by accurate paraphrasing and restating. Letting clients hear what they have said to you is a powerful way of drawing their attention to aspects that they are engaged in avoiding. Offering the conclusions you have drawn from what they have told you also invites self-challenge. For example, the practitioner might have said to Penny:

PRACTITIONER: Even though the relationship was costing you dearly in terms of your emotional and physical health, you had no choice but to stay and tolerate the situation. Is that right?

8   *Be open to challenge yourself.* The ways in which you can be open to challenge yourself are by:
   • listening non-defensively when clients point out in what ways you may have been unhelpful

- openly sharing with clients when you think the counselling process has been inhibited by collusion or competition and owning your part in that
- exploring your own behaviour in supervision and challenging yourself. In other words, do not expect clients to receive your challenge with openness, unless you are prepared to do the same.

9   *Use the challenging sequence.* We want at this point to provide some guidelines for using a sequence of reflective and probing skills in challenging. First, we offer an example to illustrate how these skills are used in challenging a client.

Dave is someone who has been having problems at work with his team. Junior colleagues are scared of him and dislike having to approach him. In the words of his referring line manager, Dave is 'a grievance waiting to happen'. Dave sees himself as honest and straightforward in his dealings with others. His practitioner, on the other hand, experiences him rather differently. Her view is that he comes across as critical, negative and anxious about getting things right. Her aim, therefore, is to encourage him to explore his behaviour and view it from a different perspective.

PRACTITIONER: So, saying what you think honestly and directly sounds important for you. [*paraphrase*]

DAVE: Yes, it is. People expect it . . . and anyway, if they can't take the truth, they shouldn't ask. The truth never hurt anyone and constructive criticism is important.

PRACTITIONER: When you said 'take the truth', it sounds like you expect honesty to be painful. [*paraphrase to focus on what client was implying*]

DAVE: [*with a hollow laugh and avoiding direct comment on the practitioner's paraphrase*] I say what I think when I'm asked. At work yesterday, a colleague asked me what I thought of a report she'd written and I told her straight that I thought it was disappointing. I pointed out where it was too superficial. She didn't like it much but that was my honest opinion.

PRACTITIONER: Dave, from the way you described the feedback you gave your colleague, it sounded to me like you focused on what was wrong with her report. I wonder whether she experienced your 'straight talking' and honesty as criticism and was hurt. Does that make any sense to you? [*summarises to check that she has understood her client and to offer her perspective. She ends with a tentative question to encourage Dave to stay involved in the exploration.*]

DAVE: She asked me what I thought of it and I told her – tears won't make it any different!

COUNSELLOR: [*noticing that Dave has ignored her challenge*] And there was nothing good in the report then – it was poor. [*uses a statement to focus on what Dave had implied*]

DAVE:No! Of course not – some parts of it were good. In fact, some bits were excellent but . . . I was going to say, 'That's not straight feedback' but of course it is.

COUNSELLOR: From what you've said so far, it sounds to me like giving honest feedback usually involves you being critical. Is that worth exploring further, do you think?

The skills outlined in earlier chapters can be used in different combinations and sequences to challenge. It is also important to remember that simply stringing basic skills together does not develop effective challenges. Your perspectives will be based on careful listening and attention to your clients and will be explainable in terms of whichever counselling theory you espouse. Several other books in the 'Counselling in Action' series provide different theoretical perspectives which you might use to assist your understanding of what clients bring. Of course, supervision also provides an opportunity for exploring how and in what areas to challenge clients.

Guidelines for using skills to challenge:

1   Identify the client's core messages and paraphrase to check and show understanding.
2   Add your understanding of the meaning of the client's messages in a short summary or a statement.
3   Return the focus to your client. When you give a client your perspective or interpretation you temporarily move the focus to yourself. It is important that you end by asking clients for their reactions. You might say something like:
    • How does that sound to you?
    • Does that make any sense as a way of looking at what you've experienced?
    • What do you think about what I've just said?
    • How do you feel now about what I've just said?

Types of Challenge

So far in this chapter we have discussed challenging as a general strategy, identifying some of the areas where you might usefully challenge clients, and have offered some general guidelines for the manner in which you might challenge. There are, however, a number of distinct challenging strategies and it is to these that we now want to turn.

Confrontation

To confront means, among other things, to encounter or to be face to face with. Specifically, we are using the term to mean helping clients to identify and face the games, distortions, ruses and discrepancies which keep them from effective change. Confrontation is a strategy that uses both reflective and probing skills to call clients' attention to perceived incongruities, inconsistencies or 'camouflage' that they are using to deceive themselves.

People often become clients because they do not think there is any way out of their problems. Certainly, all problems have something of an impasse in them, otherwise they would not be problems. Nevertheless, clients are often unaware or only dimly aware of how they disempower themselves. Your task in confronting clients is to help them to discover how they do this and to reclaim their personal power.

Consider the following example. A client, Anna, was exploring a work relationship. Her colleague was continually letting her down, by not turning up, working from home and yet not completing tasks. She revealed that she covered for him, taking work from him so that customers wouldn't be let down. She was angry and resentful. The counsellor thought she was rescuing him and indulging him.

> PRACTITIONER: You sound furious with him and you bail him out regularly, it seems.
>
> ANNA: [*angrily*] I can't just do nothing when he doesn't turn up. Other people are being let down and it causes problems. I'm also responsible for some customers and I just can't leave work undone, calls not followed up.
>
> PRACTITIONER: You say you 'can't do nothing'. What do you imagine would happen if you did just that?
>
> ANNA: Well, I suppose customers would complain and the department would get a bad name, we might lose business . . . and I haven't thought any further than that.

PRACTITIONER: So, you're protecting everyone, the department and customers and letting him 'off the hook' too.

ANNA: I'm being responsible. There's nothing wrong with that, is there? You're suggesting that when he makes a blunder or a mess, I should let him sort it out, are you? Well, that won't work!

PRACTITIONER: I'm not suggesting anything. What would be so unworkable or unacceptable about letting him sort his mistakes out?

ANNA: [*sheepishly*] I suppose he'd sort his blunders out. He'd have to. I get a real 'high' out of being efficient and, I don't know, being *the* person who can sort things out and get things moving.

PRACTITIONER: And you won't be needed or quite so much if you stop rescuing him?

ANNA: [*subdued*] Sounds awful to admit but I do enjoy the praise and the accolades. It makes the frustration seem not so bad. I want to be responsible but I'm fed up with doing his job as well as my own *and* no one is asking me to.

Anna's view of the problem was 'distorted'. The counsellor's confrontation helped her to realise that she had a choice about how much she helped her colleague. She could be efficient and responsible without rescuing. Her value to colleagues wasn't dependent on her 'bailing others out'.

Confronting discrepancies and inconsistencies

Clients may, with or without awareness, present you with discrepant messages. Discrepancies may be between:

- clients' views of themselves and how others see them
- how clients are and what they wish to be
- clients' verbal and non-verbal behaviour
- what clients say they want and what they are doing to get it.

Here are some brief examples and possible responses:

- Catherine says she is happy in her relationship, yet she looks downcast and sits with her arms folded and fists clenched.

  PRACTITIONER: Catherine, I'm aware that when we've talked about your *partner*, you've looked very dejected and unhappy.

- Jack says everything at work is fine with a snigger and a hollow laugh.

    PRACTITIONER: Jack, what would that snigger say?

- Eileen says that she finds counselling helpful and is often late for her appointments.

    PRACTITIONER: Eileen, I'm pleased that you're finding this helpful. I've noticed that you've been late several times. I imagine that you're also finding it difficult.

Let us see how a discrepancy between what a client says he wants and what he is doing to achieve it might be confronted.

The client, Ray, who is in his forties, is discussing his work future.

    RAY: [*slowly and forcefully*] I'd really like to give up my job and buy a smallholding somewhere. I'd like to live in the country and . . . not exactly be self-sufficient . . . but make my living by doing some freelance work and develop my furniture-making skills. I keep looking at the price of property and it's still rising. I hope it comes off. I've wanted this for some time – it's a dream. It keeps me going when I'm driving up and down the motorway.
    PRACTITIONER: Ray, you said 'I hope it comes off.' It's as if you're telling me that getting what you want is dependent on hope rather than anything you can do. I'm not sure if that's what you meant.
    RAY: That's right, I haven't done anything yet. I am hopeful though – to keep me going. Because if I find out it's impossible, then I won't have anything much to look forward to.

The counsellor focuses on an apparent contradiction. Ray is expressing keenness but doing nothing. Her challenge prompted a realisation that in keeping his plans as 'dreams', he was protecting himself from the possibility of disappointment.

You may also confront the following 'protective devices' that clients use to explain their positions without facing the hurt. These include:

1 *Rationalising.* Clients may excuse or justify their positions by diminishing the importance of their concerns. For example, Brian, who was out of work and struggling financially, told his practitioner that he was

glad this had happened to him because he could now talk much more sympathetically to others with problems.

2   *Delaying.* Some clients will avoid accepting the urgency of a situation because the possible outcomes are costly or frightening. Paula, for example, was pregnant and had recently separated from her partner. She had 'known' for several weeks before consulting her doctor that she was pregnant. She was very ambivalent about having a child and was considering a termination. By delaying, she would not have to face making a decision.

3   *Not 'owning' the problem.* Clients may blame others or focus on changes that others need to make. It may well be that, if the other people in the situation acted differently, then the problem might be resolved or overcome. However, clients can use this to avoid taking action themselves. For example, Rosemary was talking about her level of work stress. She told the practitioner that colleagues were demanding and insensitive to her. They had no interest in knowing about the pressure that she was under and probably wouldn't do anything to help her even if they did know.

Confronting strengths

Clients often have strengths and resources that they overlook. Acknowledging their strengths can help clients to understand themselves differently. The following example illustrates this.

A client, Brenda, was recently promoted to personal assistant to a company director. She was not coping well and felt very anxious. She revealed that her boss was unhappy with her work and that he had alerted Human Resources. Her job had grown since she had taken it because her boss had taken on new responsibilities. She described him as 'a lovely man' whom everyone respected. She had recently moved house on the strength of her promotion and feared that if she lost this job it would mean less money and losing her house and garden that she loved. She lived alone and said that she felt unsupported in her life.

PRACTITIONER: You don't have support at home or at work from what you've said. It sounds like your boss expects you to deal with whatever comes up.

BRENDA: [*angrily*] No, I'm not supported. He never tells me what to do. He never says what is a priority and what isn't. He complains that I'm not

> quick enough and yet he expects me to listen . . . to sit and talk for ages.
> I get no guidance because he's not there half the time. One of the other
> secretaries said the way to handle him is to cosset him!

PRACTITIONER: You're angry with him and don't sound like you want to cosset
him. From what you've said so far, you seem to have shown initiative
and ability in getting things for yourself – a new job, a new home, a
garden which you are looking forward to organising. I may be wrong
but I don't hear you talking about using your initiative with your boss.

BRENDA: Yes! You're right. I do have initiative.

PRACTITIONER: And you're waiting for him to tell you what to do.

BRENDA: That's not using my initiative, is it?

Brenda then went on to explore what she would like her work life to be like; how she could develop a work plan to submit to her boss rather than ask him to plan with her or for her. She thought that, if her work situation did not improve, she would leave as soon as she found another job, knowing that she had done what she could to effect change.

The practitioner helped Brenda to focus on a strength that she was not using. She challenged in a tentative way by using paraphrasing and checking statements before offering her own perspective. Brenda began to see a way out of what previously seemed to her a hopeless situation.

The following questioning approach, used extensively in solution-focused and brief therapies, is helpful for challenging clients to review both the strengths they have and how they have used these resources in the past.

Questions such as:

- When you faced similar decisions in the past, how did you resolve them?
- How could you do that again?
- What other demanding situations have you handled?
- How do you typically approach finding solutions to difficult decisions?
- When you have been anxious, yet taken a risk, what was the first small step you took to tackle the problem?

Self-confrontation

Finally, you may want to encourage clients to confront themselves in a responsible way, as an alternative to self-blame. Blame is often the acceptable face of despair. Some clients may punish themselves and self-blame in ways that rarely promote insight. You might ask them to talk to themselves as a person who is interested in understanding rather than condemning might. Consider the following example:

DAVE: I never learn. It's like I'm on automatic pilot. It's not as if I don't know what to do. But, instead of saying 'No', I grin like a clown and say 'Yes'. So now I'm lumbered again. I'm doing something I don't want to do and I'm angry with myself for being spineless.

PRACTITIONER: You sound hard on yourself. What would someone say to you if they were commenting on your actions in a more understanding way?

DAVE: I don't know . . . I suppose they'd say, 'You made a mistake. You knew what you wanted to do and you didn't do it. You ignored yourself again and now you're feeling resentful.' As I was saying 'Yes', I thought, 'I don't *want* to do this, but I *ought* to help out. It's mean not to.'

PRACTITIONER: Refusing requests is being mean, is it?

The invitation to Dave to talk from a more understanding perspective helps him to shift from blame to greater self-understanding. He now has a better idea of how he sabotages his attempts to say what he wants.

We have discussed some of the different ways in which confronting enables you to challenge clients. We now want to look at how providing clients with feedback constitutes another strategy for challenging.

Giving feedback

Giving feedback challenges clients' self-understanding by providing them with information about how another, the practitioner, experiences them. Consider the following example.

A client, Christopher, is facing an important interview for a training course. He is concerned that he will not be able to answer his interviewers well enough to obtain a place. He has talked clearly and sensibly about the preparation he has done and the way he will tackle the interview.

CHRISTOPHER: The problem is that I get muddled and my mind goes blank. I don't seem to be able to get my thoughts in order.

The practitioner decides to challenge by giving Christopher some feedback.

PRACTITIONER: You've given me a very clear outline of what you've done to prepare for the interview. You've also stated how you will handle certain questions, if asked. And you're telling me you can't think. It seems to me you're thinking very clearly.

Christopher's view of his behaviour is at odds with the way he is actually behaving. The practitioner's view helps him to begin to see his behaviour in a different light. He also begins to explore how he undermines himself by believing that he is a 'muddled thinker'.

Guidelines for giving feedback

The following guidelines were developed by Hopson and Scally (1982).

1 *Describe the behaviour not the client.* For example, being called manipulative or insensitive is both attacking and unhelpful. Clients are likely to want to defend themselves rather than listen. Describe the clients' behaviour rather than labelling them. For example, instead of:

PRACTITIONER: You're a possessive person – which is probably why your children don't confide in you,

you might say something like:

PRACTITIONER: I notice you sounded hurt when you described your children as secretive. I wonder if they see you as intruding on their space. What do you think?

2 *Be concrete.* Describe your client's behaviour clearly and specifically. For example, simply telling clients that they are being resistant does not give them any indication of what they are doing and what they might change.
3 *Own your feedback.* This means saying what you think and feel and owning it as such. Begin your feedback with some of the statements outlined in Chapter 3 such as 'I notice', 'I think' or 'I feel'.
4 *Do not blame or condemn.* State clearly what you think and describe the consequences of the client's behaviour. Feedback, as illustrated in the following example, would be attacking rather than challenging:

PRACTITIONER: You don't easily express your feelings here. If that is what you do at home, then it's no surprise to me that your marriage is so unsatisfactory. Perhaps if you started being more open and less rigid, you would be more at ease with your wife.

Put without blame, it might sound something like this:

PRACTITIONER: I'm aware that you are prepared to talk thoughtfully about what you do, but you don't say how you feel or express your feelings. I find it hard to know what's really important for you and I wonder if your wife does too?

5   *Offer positive as well as negative feedback.* Clients can begin to handle their problems better by doing more of what is positive rather than concentrating solely on eliminating the negative. Giving balanced feedback will help clients towards a clearer appreciation of their resources and strengths as well as their deficits. That does not mean prefacing feedback with hollow praise. We find that balanced feedback is particularly helpful with clients who escalate or 'catastrophise' their problems, for example:

CLIENT: It's absolutely disgraceful – how can I possibly go for an interview when I'm feeling like this? How can they expect to get the best out of me when I've only had a week to prepare? At this rate I'll never move on!

PRACTITIONER: From my experience of you, you seem skilled and practised at coping well under pressure. You're proud of being well organised and focused. I'm interested that you're finding this interview a daunting prospect.

6   *Check that clients have heard your feedback.* Invite them to take part in an exploration of what you have said.

Giving information

Clients may lack information that would help them to reassess their concerns. Let us consider the following examples.

A bereaved client, Daphne, says that she cannot understand her reactions; her feelings are so intense and sometimes so negative. Giving her some information about what typically happens to those who are bereaved, along with some notion of the tasks which individuals face, may help Daphne to understand herself in the process. She may then feel more able to express what she feels without so much guilt and self-deprecation.

Richard is a trainee on a counselling course. He is finding some of the practical work difficult and is anxious that he will fail. The following information might well help him:

- what students typically feel at this stage in the course
- what problems students confront when they attempt to integrate skills into their own style
- a discussion of his past grades and feedback about how he is seen by those who will assess him
- how many students withdraw or fail.

Information may help clients to see themselves and their concerns differently. The student in the preceding example came for a tutorial thinking he was a failure. Exploring the information he was given helped Richard to see himself as someone who was confronting the typical problems that accompany a skills training. The information also helped him to focus on which aspects of his counselling performance he could usefully improve.

Guidelines for providing information

1 *Make sure the information is relevant.* For example, the student Richard does not need information on drop-out rates from undergraduate courses.

2 *Do not overload the client with detail.* There is a limit to what people can remember and assimilate.

3 *Make sure the client understands what you are saying.* Therefore, present the information clearly, avoid jargon and invite questions. You might want to ask clients to summarise what you have said.

4 *Help the client to use the information.* Information of itself does not solve problems. For example, simply telling clients about a transition model or the tasks facing them at this particular developmental stage in their lives will not make them more skilled, or more competent to deal with their concerns. You may need to help clients to see the relevance of the information and to explore what new light it throws on their concerns.

5   *Do not confuse information with advice.* Giving information is not the same as voicing your opinion about the action that clients should take. Recommending or advising may have a place in counselling. We don't think there is anything wrong with giving clear, relevant suggestions based on your knowledge of a particular client and your expertise. For example advising a client who is complaining of being harassed at work to keep a detailed log of all the incidents would seem appropriate.

Giving directives

Directives are the most influencing of all the challenging strategies. As the description suggests, the counsellor openly directs the client to do something. This skill is characteristically used in the Middle Stage when the practitioner has made some assessment as to what it would be most useful to direct the client to do. Directives are intended to guide clients to areas that the practitioner believes will be a fruitful source for deeper understanding. The following example demonstrates how giving directives challenges clients.

A client, Peter, is talking about being excluded by his partner. He recounts, in a level and balanced way, what to the practitioner seem hurtful experiences.

PRACTITIONER: *[gently]* Peter, put some feelings to those words. *[gives a directive]*

PETER: I don't know, hurt and sad, I suppose

PRACTITIONER: Stay with those feelings for a moment; experience what you feel. *[gives another directive]*

PETER: *[sits quietly for a moment]* Actually, I feel angry. As I think about what he did and how insensitive he's been, *[much louder]* I feel really furious. How could he be so inconsiderate?

Here the practitioner uses directives to help Peter articulate what he feels. He shifts from not displaying much emotion to describing and expressing his feelings.

Clients often give clues in the language they use as to how they avoid taking responsibility for themselves and deny their ability to change. For example, they may say 'I can't', 'I have to' or 'I should'. In each instance, you may direct them by inviting them to experience saying, 'I won't', 'I choose to' or 'I want to' respectively.

Guidelines for giving directives

1   *Do not overuse.* Clients may feel persecuted, if they are constantly on the receiving end of directives. Too liberal a use can rob clients of control and may encourage dependence.

2   *Be clear about your intentions.* Before you direct clients, ask yourself whether doing this will help them to see their concerns from a different and more liberating angle.

3   *Check with clients first.* You can ask clients if they would be willing, for example, to do an exercise or a role-play.

4   *Be prepared for clients to say 'No!'* Clients may resist doing what you ask. If this occurs, you may want to explore what they experienced in the interchange. You may need to accept that you have been heavy-handed or intrusive. Trust may be an issue here. Clients may not trust that you will be able to offer them the protection that they think they will need; or they may not trust that the technique you are suggesting will help them.

5   *Keep your voice calm and direct.* Saying, 'Put some words to that feeling' in a stentorian tone may well either antagonise or frighten clients.

6   *Give clear instructions.* A practitioner reported that she asked a client to take himself back to when he was nine years old. She said 'Take your time and think your way into your childhood, *a bit.*' The client did just that. He thought a bit, then said the exercise was difficult and did not want to do it. Clearer instructions would have been something like, 'I want you to imagine that you are nine years old. Now take your time. Sit as you imagine you sat when you were little. When you are ready, look down and describe what you are wearing.' Here the practitioner gives the client space and some clear guidelines that help him to begin to relive a time when he was small.

Self-disclosure or self-sharing

This strategy occurs when, in order to promote new awareness, you share some experiences of your own life with your client. It has its basis in empathic understanding and is not the same as telling clients that you 'know exactly how they feel because something similar has happened' to you.

Self-disclosure shifts the focus from client to practitioner and for that reason is best used sparingly. The counselling relationship is one of limited reciprocity and dwelling for too long on your own material is inappropriate. In one sense, of course, you cannot avoid disclosing yourself to clients, both by your self-presentation and what you say and do. Before offering some guidelines for self-disclosure, we want to look briefly at two examples and identify in what way self-disclosure both challenges, and promotes new awareness.

Example 1

Beverley is discussing her work. She has taken a job that she dislikes intensely and from which she is attempting to escape.

> BEVERLEY: It's as if I've gone against what I ought to do by taking this job. I feel as if I've rebelled and now I'm paying for it. They were right all along.
>
> PRACTITIONER: You haven't done what your parents wanted, is that it?
>
> BEVERLEY: I can't remember them ever saying I should do this or that. They used to say, 'The important thing is that you're happy.'
>
> PRACTITIONER: My parents used to say to me, 'Do whatever you like. It's all right by us', and I understood that what they really meant was 'as long as it involves being in a profession'. Does that make any sense to you?
>
> BEVERLEY: That's it exactly. When you said that, I realised that this job wasn't a step up the ladder, more money and responsibility, in other words, none of the things they would approve of. They've never said that in so many words but that is what they wanted for me. I've rebelled against them, haven't I? And at my age, I don't know why I continually seem to do that!

The practitioner's self-disclosure was short and relevant. She responded to Beverley's comment about what she 'ought' to have done. Instead of questioning, she considered that an example from her own life might help Beverley to begin to understand her behaviour in a different way.

Example 2

Simon is putting a brave face on his misery. He is being stalwart in describing a particularly painful episode. In response to the practitioner's statement, 'I imagine you felt sad', Simon continues with:

SIMON: [regretfully] These things happen, don't they? That's life . . . and you just have to get on with it. Dwelling on the past won't change anything. Neither will moaning on about it.

The practitioner notices that Simon has avoided talking about or expressing his feelings. Furthermore, he has distanced himself from the issue by saying 'you' when he is actually referring to himself. Instead of using a directive, such as 'Will you say "I'm going to get on with life"?' or a paraphrase, such as 'You want to get on with life and not be hampered by feelings', she decides that self-disclosure may help him to express what he is hinting at:

PRACTITIONER: I think that, if I'd experienced the rejection that you've experienced, I would feel sad and hurt. I've also wanted to ignore painful feelings. I wonder if that is how it is for you?
SIMON: I suppose I don't want to seem weak and – don't laugh – but I think that if, I got really sad, I would never be able to stop. I'd never be happy again. I do feel awful, especially at night.

Here the practitioner used self-disclosure to model talking about feelings. Sometimes clients lack the skill of making feeling statements. They have had little practice at identifying, labelling and expressing their feelings. They lack what Steiner (1997) calls 'emotional literacy'. The practitioner's self-disclosure enabled Simon to feel safe enough to begin to explore his feelings.

Guidelines for self-disclosure

1 *Understand your client first.* You will be in a position to self-disclose effectively, if you have a clear understanding of how clients see their concerns and have considered what they may be implying or overlooking.
2 *Consider the impact.* Disclosure about your failures to cope may make you seem inexpert and unsafe to clients. Conversely, revealing your triumphs may daunt clients who are striving to make small changes.
3 *Be clear about your intentions.* Your aim is to assist the client. If you are disclosing to unburden yourself, gain sympathy or to relieve your own

feelings, then it is more appropriately discussed either in supervision or in counselling for yourself (Hawkins and Shohet, 2000).

4   *Be brief.* Talking at length about yourself takes the focus from clients and may burden or bore. It may also collude with avoidance behaviour, giving those who want to steer clear of talking about themselves a loophole.

5   *Tailor your self-disclosure.* By this we mean use experiences with which clients can identify. Telling a client who is in debt and struggling that you understand what it is like to be short of money '. . . *because £30,000 per year really doesn't go anywhere irrespective of what some people* think . . .' does not show much understanding of the client's world and is unhelpful.

6   *Be direct.* Use 'I' and describe the experience clearly and directly. End your statement by returning the focus to your client.

Finally, let us turn now to a strategy that invites challenges by focusing on what is happening in the relationship between you and your clients, a strategy that often feels risky and yet is surprisingly powerful.

Immediacy

Immediacy means focusing on the 'here and now' of the counselling conversation. Clients will not only talk about past and current events in their lives and what has happened outside the counselling room but they will also speculate about the future, and certainly goal setting and action planning are future orientated. The space for reviewing the past and considering the future is the present; these issues cannot be discussed anywhere else. However, clients may not be aware of how they are feeling 'right now'. They may gain new awareness by staying with and exploring their thoughts and feelings as they occur 'now' in relation to you and to what they are revealing. Let us look at an example of immediacy. The practitioner is attempting to enable a client to focus on what is going on for her now.

The client, Diana, was talking about how she would cope with a forthcoming important event at work. She was describing, in a bombastic way, how she would handle the meeting. The practitioner thought that the brusque words might be a mask for fear. Certainly, the client had talked about 'getting in first'.

DIANA: [*with a sigh*] I'll just say what I think and, if they don't like it, well that's too bad!

PRACTITIONER: You seemed deflated as you said that and I wonder what you're feeling now?

DIANA: Do I? Well, my stomach's churning a bit!

PRACTITIONER: Hm! without power – almost defeated. [*Diana nods.*] What are you feeling at this moment?

DIANA: Scared if you want to know! I can see their faces and the grey suits. Hear the questions and the 'put downs'. When I reply, it's as if I know nothing and I'm talking incoherently . . . [*begins to cry*] Whatever I say will be wrong.

PRACTITIONER: Sounds like you see yourself on trial and you're frightened of the verdict. [*Client nods.*] What are you saying to yourself now?

DIANA: [*thoughtfully and slowly*] I'm a failure . . . useless and I don't deserve to succeed. They all know more than me and I'll show my ignorance. I won't be able to control my fear.

Diana went on to explore her thoughts. The practitioner asked her to compare her frightening fantasy with what had actually happened so far in her work life. Diana was able to gain a more objective view of herself as someone who was knowledgeable and had achieved. She realised that, though collectively a committee might have greater breadth of knowledge than her, that did not make her stupid or a failure.

Immediacy can also be used to focus on the relationship between practitioner and client. Exploring what occurs in the counselling relationship may help clients to gain a clearer understanding of what happens in their other relationships. You may explore what is happening at the moment between you and your clients or what you discern as patterns that you see emerging. The latter is often described as 'relationship immediacy' (Egan, 2002). Let us look at an example of relationship immediacy.

A client, Harry, is talking about supporting others, especially his mother who has a disability, and his girlfriend. He says that one of his strengths is being able to listen to others and gain their confidence. The practitioner thinks that he supports others at a cost to himself. He is looking tired and has not wanted to focus on himself. He is prepared to talk about what he does.

PRACTITIONER: I'm thinking, 'I wonder who supports you?'

HARRY: [*sharply*] I've got friends, you know that. Anyway, [*with a hostile smile*] isn't this what counselling's all about, you listening to me?

PRACTITIONER: I think you're telling me that talking about support for yourself is a 'no-go area'.

HARRY: It's not that. Other people have got enough on their plates without listening to me all day. It's not as if I'm very depressed or redundant or homeless, is it? You know, in dire straits?

PRACTITIONER: I don't think receiving support is conditional on severe problems. I'd like to say what I think happens between us. I've noticed that you find it hard to receive support from me to the extent that you cover your feelings of hurt with either anger or a joke. I notice that if I really try to understand you, you push me away with a laugh or throw-away line. Perhaps, I've moved in too close too quickly and not respected your pace enough. Does what I've said make any sense to you?

HARRY: Sometimes you really understand me and I feel caught out! I feel anxious telling you this, because I know it isn't true . . . but it's like you can see right through me and see that I'm cowardly. So, I guess I avoid sharing what I think and feel. Sometimes you push me and I don't like that.

The practitioner uses immediacy to focus on a pattern. Harry continues by saying that wanting support is like an 'admission of frailty'. He also feels vulnerable in stating his wants because that means getting closer to people who might then reject him. Being strong and not asking for help is a safer option.

When to use immediacy

1 *When trust is an issue.* Clients may not be engaging in the counselling process because they do not see the practitioner as trustworthy or they are anxious about forming a close, trusting relationship. For example, Wendy believes that, if she shows how distressed she is, the practitioner will not be able to cope.

> PRACTITIONER: Wendy, I sense you don't feel safe enough with me to let me see how unhappy you are. I wonder what you imagine would happen between us, if you shared your sadness.

2 *When the counselling is circular.* Consider the following example. A client, Rachel, was talking about her partner and whether or not they would live together. The practitioner became aware that she was feeling detached and the conversation was coming back to the same point,

whether Rachel could raise the issue with her partner or wait for him to make the first move.

PRACTITIONER: Rachel, I'm aware that I'm feeling uninvolved. I've realised that we're talking over the same ground. It's as if we're circling and my hunch is we're not getting near what's really significant for you. What's your view?

3   *When there are boundary issues.* Clients may want the counselling relationship to spill over into a friendship. The counselling relationship is often characterised by mutual affection and respect. It is not unusual for clients to fantasise about romantic relationships with their practitioners. This becomes problematic if these fantasies are acted upon (Bond, 2000; Yalom, 2001; McLeod, 2003). If you think this is happening, then you will need to talk about it with your client and reaffirm the boundaries. For example:

KEITH: I think we get on so well together. It's a shame we only meet up once a week. Perhaps we could go for a drink some time or I could buy you dinner – as a kind of thank you for listening to all this boring detail. We could talk about other things than my problems with access to my children.

PRACTITIONER: Keith, I have a lot of respect for the way you're handling a very difficult situation and I'm not aware of being bored. I appreciate your invitation. And I think it's important for both of us that our relationship remains on a professional footing. Perhaps that's an issue for us to talk about now. What do you think?

4   *When there is an 'impasse'.* An impasse is a kind of 'gridlock' where there seems little prospect of movement. Sometimes an impasse occurs because the problem has been defined as insoluble or, more usually, because clients are experiencing strong internal conflicts. Yvonne wanted to leave home and yet she couldn't. She felt frustrated and angry with the practitioner for not helping her.

PRACTITIONER: Yvonne, I'm aware of wanting to make a difficult decision easy for you. You seem to be angry because you see my interventions as pressurising you and dismissing your concerns. We seem to be stuck. I wonder what we'd see if we were able to observe what was happening now between us. Any thoughts?

Guidelines for immediacy

1   *Be assertive.* Say directly what you think, feel and observe.
2   *Be open yourself.* Immediacy is not pointing out the unproductive aspects of their behaviour to clients. If a pattern is developing between you and clients – for example, a pattern of avoidance or collusion or cosiness – then you have some part in that.
3   *Describe what you think is happening clearly and specifically.* Say what you think is happening, what you observe the client doing and what you are doing.
4   *Ask the client to comment on what you have said.*

Finally, the power of immediacy is that it enables you to 'capture the moment' and focus on what is happening as it occurs. It also faces both of you with the dynamics of your relationship and may provide clients with the different experience of dealing with issues in a non-defensive way, as they arise.

What happens if you do not challenge clients?

Reassessment by challenging is a process and rarely a 'one-off'. It takes time and involves gradual 'cognitive shifts' for clients. Failure to challenge may mean that counselling becomes aimless and clients do not gain the new insights essential for goal setting and change. In one sense, the counselling process is challenging from the outset because clients are brought face-to-face with their concerns from the start. However, unless you influence clients to adopt different perspectives, they are unlikely to move beyond their present limiting views – those views that are keeping them stuck or immobilised. Challenging is demanding and requires clients to look differently at themselves and their concerns as a necessary precursor to change.

Communicating Core Values

In Chapter 4 we discussed the core values as the bedrock of counselling help, qualities that permeate the entire process and are essentially not stage-specific. When challenging your clients to take the risk of considering alternatives or revealing aspects of themselves, you are both moving to a position of increased vulnerability. Your ability to be congruent and to communicate your acceptance and empathy is significant in differentiating challenges that are containing yet robust from those that are harsh and uncaring.

Summary

This chapter has been about challenging, the purpose of which is to enable clients to 'go below the surface' or to the 'edge of their awareness'. Exploring more deeply and articulating those aspects of themselves and their concerns about which they are either unaware or dimly aware brings new information into the frame. The outcome of using the challenging strategies is that clients will have different and more empowering perspectives on their concerns. In effect, they will have reassessed their position.

Reassessment is not an end in itself. It is useful in so far as it enables clients to see possibilities for change and to stand on the threshold of action. Some clients may leave counselling, having adopted a different perspective on themselves and their concerns. That is sufficient motivation for them to change or to take action. Others may need help to decide precisely what they want to change and to plan how to effect that change. The next chapter discusses goal setting and action planning.

6

THE ENDING STAGE
Action and Closure

The Ending Stage

Aims (the intended outcomes)
To decide on appropriate change
To implement change
To transfer learning
To end the working relationship

Strategies
Goal setting
Action planning
Evaluating action and sustaining change
Ending

Skills
The foundation skills used in the basic sequences
for exploring and challenging

In this chapter, we begin by discussing the aims of the Ending Stage and continue by reviewing the strategies by which these aims will be achieved. We will concentrate more on strategies than on skills because, once you have mastered the basic skill sequences which enable you to facilitate exploration and reassessment, you will be well equipped to assist clients in the process of setting goals, planning and taking appropriate action (Munro et al., 1989).

The Ending Stage typically deals with goals, action and ending or closure. As a result of the work done in the two preceding stages, clients will have gained the kind of clearer understanding, both of themselves and of their concerns, that provides the impetus for change. Planning and taking effective action are made more possible because of the work done in the Beginning and Middle Stages. Some clients, of course, may choose not to travel any further with you. Once they have explored their problems and gained a new view, they see clearly what they want to do and set about achieving it. Others will need help to decide what change they want and your support while they try out new behaviours. For some, this is the most significant stage. If clients have a history of difficulty converting intentions into successful actions, this stage provides an opportunity for them to understand their difficulties and to adopt different ways of making decisions and implementing actions.

Aims

We have identified above the four aims to guide the work of the Ending Stage. Let us look at these in turn.

To decide on appropriate change

If clients are to cope more effectively with their concerns or solve their problems, they will need to do two things: first, they will need to identify the specific changes they want to make; and second, they will need to check that those changes will have the particular impact that they want on their problems. The fact that clients have explored and reassessed their concerns usually means that they are inclined towards change and can see the desirability of action. However, that does not necessarily mean that they will know precisely what change they want to make; nor does it mean that they know how to implement that change. To assume otherwise risks overlooking an important step in the helping process. Changing generally involves risks and losses as well as benefits and gains. In addition to identifying what positive outcomes they seek, you will need to help your clients to decide what risks and costs are manageable for them. Helping clients to decide on changes that are appropriate for them involves helping them to identify positive outcomes that are both within their resources and have acceptable costs and benefits. Some clients may select goals and choose actions that involve major changes to their lives. Others may wish to proceed more cautiously. Neither option is necessarily better than the other. The best choices are the ones to which the client feels committed and well placed to implement.

To implement change

This may sound obvious but clients must act if they want to change. They must stop doing some things and start doing others. For example, clients who want to build their confidence will need to change their habits in some way. Your task will be to help clients both to decide on what action to take and to take that action. This involves exploring different options, choosing ones which seem appropriate, as well as timing and sequencing any action. Occasionally, you may want to use rehearsal or engage in some role-play with clients as a preparation.

To transfer learning

Through the processes of exploration and challenging, clients learn about aspects of themselves and their behaviour. The ultimate goal is to convert these insights into actions. This may involve working through successive sub-goals of incremental difficulty. The first changes may begin with the client implementing changes in the relative safety of the helping relationship where encouragement and feedback can be given. This is a safe place to experiment, because mistakes will not carry the kind of adverse consequences that they might in other areas of the client's life. The next challenge is implementing these changes as actions outside the helping relationship. This can be scary if clients lack confidence or there is a lot at stake. Success at this stage means that clients are well placed to transfer their new knowledge and skills to other situations. A good experience of the Ending Stage will often result in clients acquiring skills that are not only relevant to the issues for which they sought help but are also transferable to other situations. Consider the following examples.

Rod learned to express his feelings appropriately. His practitioner helped Rod to explore not only how he denied his feelings but typically when and with whom. In order to enable him to transfer his learning about himself and the new skills he had acquired, they explored how he might confront situations both at work and at home in a more appropriate way. They started this process with Rod expressing feelings that he had previously had about his relationship with his practitioner, both positive and negative.

Gina discovered that her resentment with her partner had much to do with her tendency to rescue him. She used the opportunity to discuss her frustration and to explore ways of relating to her partner which did not involve treating him as a helpless victim, even when he solicited it. Gina also realised that her tendency to take over and to act as though others could not manage was a pattern in her life. She was able to transfer her new learning not only to her interactions with her partner but also to other relationships.

Helping clients to transfer their learning may involve identifying obstacles to change and planning how to overcome or minimise those obstacles. Coaching clients in new behaviour can also be a relevant option.

Finally, your clients will take away a 'mental picture' of you. An internalised view of the helper will give some clients a resource that they can access when confronting future problems and decisions. A colleague revealed that he frequently asked himself what his practitioner might say to him. In doing this, he gave himself the space to think through what he wanted and so avoided doing what he thought he 'should' do. Teaching clients the model described in this book can increase their resourcefulness and confidence to respond to other challenges that may arise in future.

To end the working relationship

So far in this chapter we have concentrated on helping the clients to take action to improve their lives. The quality of the relationship between you and clients provides the foundation; clients can be greatly helped by the experience of being supported and understood. However, they may experience confusing or mixed feelings at this stage. Success in resolving the issue that prompted them to seek help comes at the price of losing the relationship with you. For some, this is unproblematic. For others, this can seem so daunting that it deters them from succeeding in order to prolong the relationship. This is most likely to be an issue for those who have been starved of supportive and constructive relationships in their lives or have had bad experiences of ending relationships. Managing the ending well helps all clients and is especially important with clients for whom the anticipation of the end evokes feelings of loss and grief or uncertainty about how they will find adequate support elsewhere.

Providing a 'good' ending involves:

- reviewing the history of working together and sharing each other's experiences
- celebrating successes
- identifying the learning gained for both of you from any difficulties in the work

- planning the ending in terms of timing and whether it will be a clear stop or some form of phased ending, perhaps by meeting less frequently
- identifying and setting in place alternative sources of support where these are required. This might include whether the client can contact the practitioner for help with any future difficulties.
- saying goodbye.

The time taken with endings may vary enormously. It may be only a few minutes at the end of the final session with a very task-focused client for whom the helping relationship is simply a means to an end. On the other hand, it may be the subject of several sessions or even the major task, where the client experiences difficulty over endings. Further suggestions about the application of the strategies and skills to ending the relationship can be found towards the end of this chapter.

Endings may also prove a sad time for practitioners. You will have grown close to clients and, even though their work with you has been completed, you will inevitably miss some of them. While it is inappropriate to burden them with your feelings, it is important nonetheless to recognise that endings mean loss for you. If indeed this is the case, you will provide good modelling for your clients by disclosing in a direct and appropriate way that you will miss them and have valued the efforts they have made to change and grow.

Of course, not all endings are a time of satisfying reflection. There may be times when clients want to end the helping relationship prematurely. They may not have achieved what they wanted despite your best efforts, perhaps because they have been reluctant to tackle their concerns. Clients may sometimes think that you are not helping them and decide they want to work with another practitioner or seek a different kind of help. Sometimes they will be proved right and do get more appropriate help elsewhere. There may be some useful learning for the practitioner in these circumstances. When a client leaves for negative reasons, it is often appropriate to affirm their decision and to express an interest in hearing how things work out for them. You may also have occasion to refer them to someone else because you feel that the issues that they bring are beyond your current experience and expertise. Attention to the ending can help to avoid the client feeling abandoned or rejected by the referral process.

Let us turn now to the strategies that are instrumental in achieving the aims of the ending stage.

Strategies

Goal setting

The work of the preceding two stages involves helping clients to understand themselves in such a way that they can see change as a possibility. Goal setting provides a strategy for helping clients both to generate and to decide the outcomes they want. It is a particularly useful strategy because it is one that clients frequently bypass, as well as being omitted in the ways that friends, work colleagues and family offer help. In these instances, goals are either assumed or taken for granted.

The tendency to pass immediately from identifying the problem to taking action omits a key step in the process, and that is to consider what goals the person concerned might have. A problem may be resolved or coped with by achieving any one of a number of different outcomes. However well you know your client or have defined the problem, it is unproductive to imagine that you either know the specific outcomes they want or the action they are prepared to take to achieve them. The identification of appropriate goals will usually be based on a combination of rational and emotional responses. In other words, clients will both know what they want and have a 'felt sense' of what is right for them (Gendlin, 1996, 2003).

Consider the following example. The client, Daniel, sought help because he was lonely. He had few friends and often felt intensely sad. He wanted his life to be different; he wanted a partner, friends and to feel valued by others. He opened his work with his practitioner by talking about his concerns, summarised as follows:

> I want to be happier. I can't remember ever being wanted. My parents separated when I was three years old and I suppose I've never learned to trust anyone. If I'd had a stable secure childhood, then I wouldn't have the problems that I have now; and I wouldn't be so lonely and depressed.

In the Beginning Stage, Daniel talked about his past. His view or frame of reference was that he was the product of his early childhood experiences; and those experiences were responsible for his current status. He wanted life to be different but did not know how to effect change. The practitioner hypothesised that Daniel had a view of himself as unlovable and of the world as a hostile place. She noticed that he found it hard to trust her and that he withdrew whenever she attempted to get close to him.

As the work progressed and their rapport deepened, the practitioner challenged Daniel. She focused on their relationship and explored with him how he seemed to want to be close to her and for her to understand him, but when she did he pulled away. Daniel understood that this was the strategy he adopted with others. He realised that intimate friendships were frightening because he risked being rejected and hurt. Daniel became aware of how, as a bewildered child, this had been important for his self-preservation, but that now he was not in such a powerless position. The practitioner also encouraged him to explore how his self-estimation stopped him being open and taking risks with others. In her interactions with him, she pointed out how he avoided hearing praise from her. They agreed that she would point out each time he ignored positive feedback from her or dismissed his achievements.

From the work of the Middle Stage, Daniel gained a different and more liberating view of himself. He modified his beliefs about himself and others. He saw how he had allowed his past to keep him stuck in loneliness. However, now he had this altered perspective, the question remained of what he wanted to accomplish and how he would accomplish it. Daniel and his practitioner turned translating his aim of 'a happier life, with close friends and a stable partnership' into goals.

Goals are *what* the client wants to achieve and a way forward that improves the present state of affairs. Action plans are concerned with *how* clients will reach their goals. In general, identifying clear outcomes helps clients to avoid undirected and ineffective action. However, sometimes acting first and reflecting on the outcomes does help clients to gain clearer ideas of what they want. For example, a client who is unhappy in his current employment may gain a clearer understanding of the satisfactions he seeks by applying for other positions and going for interviews. Testing the market may also help him to decide what change is possible. Let us turn now to the goal-setting framework.

Developing goals

If goals are to be both practicable and feasible, they will need to fulfil the following criteria. Goals should be:

- wanted by the client
- tailored by the client
- observable and assessable
- set within a realistic time frame.

Let us look at these in turn.

1   *Goals should be wanted by the client.* This means helping clients to discover what they want to achieve and which, out of all the possible
outcomes, they value most. Making changes takes time and energy, and
clients are likely to work harder for goals that are their own. They are
less likely to sustain their investment in pursuing ends which they do
not value or which they see as imposed upon them. Listen carefully for
any hints or clues that indicate clients' lack of involvement or 'ownership' in the options they mention. The following are examples of the
statements that clients might make which suggest that they are not following their own wishes, and of possible practitioner responses:

> GEOFF: My partner and I have talked about the future and she's keen that I
> take early retirement.
> PRACTITIONER: Early retirement is what your partner prefers. I'm not sure if
> that's what you want?

And where the clues might primarily be non-verbal:

> ANDREA: [*looking fed up and sounding bored*] I suppose the way out of this
> predicament is to save more money.
> PRACTITIONER: You sound as though that idea doesn't have much appeal. I
> wonder if there are other options.

Sometimes, however, clients say quite openly that what they are planning to achieve is not what they want but either what others want or
what they think they 'ought' to do. In these instances, an option is to
shift the focus of the discussion from goal setting to an exploration of
clients' 'shoulds' and 'oughts', together with the costs and benefits of
their stated outcomes.

   Another important facet of goal setting may be helping clients to
clarify their values. Goals are more likely to be achieved if they are in
keeping with clients' values. For example, a client, Victor, tells his practitioner that he has looked forward to his retirement. However, he now
faces redundancy, which means retiring two years earlier than he had
anticipated. The news has been a great shock to him. Now that he is
actually confronted with a future without work, he begins to examine
just what work means to him and what he will do without it. Clients are

more likely to review their values in times of change or transition than at other times in their lives (Sugarman, 2001). Planning change may throw into sharper relief values that clients had previously considered less significant.

However, helping clients to identify outcomes that they want does not mean that they ignore the wishes of important people in their lives. Rather it means that, if they are helped to separate out what they want from the expectations of others, they will be in a position to make an informed choice. This, in turn, is likely to have the effect of freeing them from believing that they have no other options but to do what others expect of them. Challenging clients to test out their assumptions is one way of helping them to distinguish between their own and others' expectations.

Another way is to do a simple balance sheet. For example, Anita's goal was to increase her part-time employment to full-time. Her practitioner asked her to estimate the positive and negative effects of this option as follows:

Positives	Negatives
Develop skills	Won't be in when son (aged 12) gets home from school
Feel more confident in myself	Miss seeing friends in the day
Finances improved	Don't think I'll get much help with domestic chores
Feel more independent	Partner not too keen
Feel useful	

Anita realised that, while this was an important goal for her, she did not know how her partner and son would view certain implications of her decision. Working full time would mean she had less time to devote to their home. Rearranging the domestic tasks had not been discussed in the family. It will be hard for clients to achieve their objectives if other people who are close to them either fail to support them or disrupt their efforts.

2 *Goals should be tailored by the client.* Tailoring goals means shaping them so that they become specific and realistic. Let us consider what each of these terms means.

   • *specific*: Vague goals are unlikely to lead to effective action and change. For example, a client may make a statement like, 'I can understand now how I've let work take over my life. I do want a better social life and a better balance in my life.' This is a useful starting point for tailoring goals. However, it is vague and needs refining. For example, what does a 'better balance' and a 'better social life' actually mean for this client? Unless she specifies this, how will she know what action to take and, equally importantly, how will she know when she has achieved what she wants?

The client, Linda, is in a relationship that she finds unsatisfying. She feels neglected and dismissed by Paul, her partner. Through a process of exploration and challenging, she comes to realise that she rarely says what she wants to him. She waits for him to take the lead in their decision-making and, when she does not get what she wants, tells herself that she has been too demanding. She begins by saying:

LINDA: I do want to do something about my relationship. For a start, I want to know if we've got a future together. [*Client makes a vague statement.*]

PRACTITIONER: From what you've said over the previous weeks, it sounds as if leaving the relationship is way down your list of options. If you imagine yourself getting on better with Paul, what would be happening? [*Practitioner uses a hypothetical question to encourage the client to begin to identify some options.*]

LINDA: We'd have a closer relationship. I'd be saying what I think and feel. I would take the initiative in making decisions and not wait for him to say what he wants. I realise that I've usually kept quiet about what I want and allowed him to take control of our lives. I want to say what I really think and feel. I want more influence. I want to be equal, not someone who 'tags' along and feels resentful. [*Client becomes more specific.*]

Linda has been encouraged to be clearer about what she wants to accomplish. She has tailored a more specific goal from a vague statement. The goal – to say what she wants and thinks and feels – is within her control. Linda can learn to be more direct and open. She can develop her self-awareness and self-regard, if she chooses. In doing this, she may influence Paul's attitude towards her. She realises that she has had little practice at saying what she wants and that, in order to begin to take a more active stance with Paul, she will need to develop her assertiveness skills.

Linda and her practitioner moved on to consider various options for learning and practising a more open and assertive style with Paul.

- *realistic*: A 'realistic goal' means a goal within the client's resources. It seems obvious to state that clients are unlikely to achieve their goals if they do not have the emotional, physical, financial and social resources. For example, Ben, who has a demanding job, a partner who works full-time and a young child, may not have the resources (emotional and financial) to embark on a further professional qualification requiring part-time study at the moment.

An important aspect of the Beginning and Middle Stages may be to help clients to discover what resources they do have. However, it is important that you keep this in mind when considering goals and action. Clients may overlook or underestimate the importance both of the social systems in which they live and work and of their previous experiences and achievements.

Clients' attempts to set goals for others also comes within the category of what is unrealistic. Usually, clients have little direct control over the behaviour of others; they have the most control over their own. They may well want to set goals which include changes that they want others to make. This is not to deny that some clients suffer abuse at the hands of other people. However, the focus of a realistic goal is, by definition, the client's behaviour.

Consider the following example. Freda was discussing a work colleague, Duncan. She told the practitioner how angry she was. Her goal was to give Duncan some feedback – and Freda added, 'I want him to consider me more in future.' The practitioner pointed out that Freda could express her anger and give her feedback, but this would not ensure that she would get the consideration that she wanted. The focus shifted to Freda's behaviour and what *she* could do to influence Duncan. Freda re-evaluated her contacts with him and realised that she only reported her difficulties and decided to start informing Duncan of her successes as well. Freda thought that this action might influence him to be more appreciative of her and consequently consider her views and opinions more.

This is not to deny that the behaviour of important others in clients' lives may need to change; but the clients are the ones working with you, not their friends, colleagues or lovers. Helping clients to change their own behaviour and their responses to others might well have the desired effect of prompting change in others' actions. However, the behaviour of others is less within clients' control.

You will also be concerned with the adequacy of the goals that clients set. An adequate goal is one that either resolves the problem or helps clients to handle their concerns more effectively. A client, Arthur, for example, tells his practitioner that he is often lonely and bored, he works long hours, meets very few people and has a limited social circle and, what is more, he feels unwanted. Arthur decides that he will take up cycling again. He tells his practitioner that as a teenager, he enjoyed this sport. This goal, if achieved, is unlikely to contribute appreciably to resolving Arthur's problems of overwork and finding an alternative activity. This is definitely a step in the right direction but on its own might not extend his social circle unless he also joins a club or goes on activity holidays.

You may want to ask clients the following questions: 'If you achieve this goal, how will that help you to achieve the . . . [*partnership, social life, financial security, increased self-esteem, and so on*] . . . that you say you want?'; or 'Will achieving this outcome help you to cope more effectively with your concerns?'

As a form of self-sabotage, often based on an 'out-of-conscious-awareness' wish to maintain the status quo, clients may sometimes be attracted to inadequate goals. For example, Arthur – the client who has decided to resume cycling as a way of developing a more fulfilling social life – on discovering that he does not meet new people and his social life remains barren, may simply give up and return to immersing himself in work. This action reinforces Arthur's deeply held view that any attempt to get a better social life and make more friends is hopeless. He may be predisposed to this outcome because of a deep personal belief that he is an unlovable person who will only be valued for his achievements. Confronting and changing such a deeply held belief is possible but emotionally challenging and is best taken in manageable steps as the client becomes progressively more aware of the beliefs that underpinned his previous behaviour. Deciding whether Arthur's goal is adequate is not merely a matter of considering whether it is realistic and practical within the constraints of his life, but whether it will contribute significantly to the outcomes he has identified – outcomes that will resolve the problem that prompted him to seek some help. One way of helping Arthur may be to explore his resistance to joining clubs or going on activity holidays with other cyclists, so he can gain greater insight into his beliefs and feelings and review his goals and possible actions accordingly.

Setting realistic goals means assessing whether or not the cost of achieving a particular outcome would be excessive. One way of helping clients to make this assessment is to examine the costs and benefits of achieving this goal as opposed to others. For example, Linda – the client who wanted to be more open with her partner – may need to confront the probability that the way things are 'suits' her partner. Any changes that she makes may provoke a split in the relationship. Furthermore, *she* may learn to communicate more effectively; but *he* may resolutely seek to maintain the status quo. While challenging clients to grow is an important part of counselling help, practitioners need to appreciate that some clients may not want to change in the ways that the practitioner considers appropriate. Clients may be satisfied with a relatively small alteration in their circumstances, because the price of doing otherwise seems exorbitant to them.

3   *Goals should be observable and assessable.* Goals stated in clear behavioural terms allow both you and clients to establish yardsticks for assessing what headway clients are making. Establishing criteria for assessment allows clients to assess where they are in the process and to know when their goals have been achieved. A key question for clients to consider is: 'When you have achieved your goals, in what ways will you be behaving differently to the ways in which you are behaving now?'

Consider the following example. Gareth wants an 'easier relationship' with his son. His goals are to:
– decrease the sarcasm and ridicule he uses
– distinguish between his son as a person and his son's behaviour
– give advice when his son asks for it and not before
– give his opinion as such and not as fact.

Gareth can monitor his behaviour with his son. He will know when he is being more accepting of his son's views as a substitute for sarcasm and ridicule. Others too will be able to see him behaving differently, when he is achieving these goals.

This brings us to the final criterion.

4   *Goals should be set within a realistic timeframe.* Finally, if clients are to bring about change, you will need to challenge them to plan within a

realistic time frame. Clients who make statements like, 'I'll start saving when I've finished the improvements to the house' are being vague about the time frame and may never accomplish their goals. It is better to have a specific day or date in mind. The more specific clients can be about the timing and circumstances of the proposed changes, the more likely that the change will be implemented.

The criteria we have outlined in this section will provide you with an excellent framework for working with clients to create coherent and attainable goals for an improved future.

Exploration and challenging in goal setting

Effective goal setting requires continuing exploration and challenging. It is important that clients are encouraged to express and to explore both feelings and thoughts that may arise during this stage. They may have doubts about their ability to implement and sustain action plans, particularly if they have attempted change before and failed. Helping clients to explore their fears, their vulnerability at attempting the unfamiliar and their anxieties about choosing is typically part of the process. Goal setting does not mean that the helping process becomes an emotionally barren activity, in which ratings and lists are made, pros and cons weighed up without attention to what clients may be feeling. Indeed, there is some evidence that practitioners high in empathy, warmth and genuineness are more effective in encouraging clients to become involved in goal setting than practitioners rated as lower over these dimensions (Mickelson and Stevic, 1971).

How to set goals

The Beginning and Middle Stages will help clients to see their concerns from a different angle and one which is potentially more change orientated. However, clients may still not know *what* they are going to do with this new knowledge. They may say things like: 'I do feel better about myself. I can see that I've put myself down in the past and that is how I've stopped myself from getting what I want'; or 'I'd like to have a better relationship with my son. I can see that I've been a bit hard on him.'

Having outlined, in the previous section, the criteria for feasible goals, we now consider some of the steps and techniques for helping clients to identify specifically what they want to achieve.

Helping clients to identify options

Clients are more likely to find ways of solving or coping better with their concerns if they choose from a range of options. There are a number of useful techniques that can help clients to begin to develop goals (Egan, 2002). They include:

- imagining different futures
- brainstorming
- sentence completion.

Let us look at each of these in turn.

1   *Imagining different futures.* Egan (2002) has called this 'creating new scenarios'. Using this technique involves asking clients to imagine what the future would be like if they were either controlling their problems more effectively or had resolved them. Once clients have identified a range of possible pictures of the future, they are then encouraged to review them and choose one scene to tailor into workable goals. For example, you may sometimes want to encourage clients to generate several imaginary pictures.

Consider the following. Simon is a teacher who is dissatisfied because he could not seem to control the demands his work made on him. During previous sessions, he began to see that he was responsible for the lack of boundaries he placed on his work. He wanted a balance between work and home that gave his family/social life more prominence. His 'pictures' are as follows:

(a)   'I'd be in another job. I'd be working as a computer programmer in a small software-writing firm.'

(b)   'I'd be confining all my preparation and marking to lunch hours and from 5.00 to 6.00 p.m. each evening. I'd list my priorities and stick to them.'

(c)   'I'd have a different timetable within the school, with less responsibility for pastoral work.'

(d)   'I would be doing the same amount of work in the school, but I'd be worrying less about it. I'd believe that the preparation I'd done would be good enough.'

After spending some time exploring what each of these scenarios would feel like, Simon decides that options (b) and (d) appeal most to him. He does not want to leave teaching or give up his pastoral role. Each option has been appraised for realism and effectiveness in coping with the issue that Simon presented.

2   *Brainstorming.* This technique involves asking clients to suspend critical judgement and identify as many possibilities for change as they can. For example, a client, Caroline, who wants to control her anxiety produced the following list of options:
   – be more relaxed
   – become more assertive
   – have an increased social circle and support network
   – stop inhibiting thoughts when they occur
   – have a plan which manages my time more efficiently
   – develop interests which involve other people
   – bring about a gradual decrease in solitary pursuits
   – receive praise for what I do well
   – accept negative feedback and not be depressed by it.
No doubt you will be able to increase the list. Once Caroline has decided what she will accomplish to manage her anxiety, she can then decide on action to achieve the goal. She may decide that being more relaxed and stopping negative thoughts will help substantially. There are many ways of learning to relax and Caroline will need to decide which will best suit her. For example, she could buy a commercially made relaxation tape or join a weekend workshop or an evening class in stress management. Some of her action plans may address more than one goal. Joining an evening class may increase her social circle and provide opportunities for positive feedback. This client may decide that all of these goals will help her and, with her practitioner, she can discuss which ones to go for initially. Brainstorming can be a pleasurable activity for clients because it gives them permission to talk without the usual restraints of evaluating and questioning.

Guidelines for brainstorming

- Encourage clients to think of as many options as they can and to suspend critical judgement if they begin to evaluate options.
- Record all options. Do not censor the list either overtly, by failing to record suggestions which you think are useless or unreasonable; or more subtly, by the use of non-verbal cues such as grimacing or sighing heavily.

- Prompt them by asking: 'Who do you know who manages a similar problem to yours? What do they do?'; 'What possibilities are there locally which you could tap into?', and by offering your ideas. You might say something like, 'I notice that you haven't mentioned doing . . .'
- After each prompt, allow them time to generate further ideas.
- Ask them what action steps they have rejected in the past.
- Encourage them to use their imagination in a direct way; for example, you might say, 'Imagine that you are resolving your problem and this time you are doing something completely different; what are you doing?'
- Reward and support clients by giving positive feedback for their creativity and the energy they are putting into the exercise.
- Make it pleasurable. We do not mean trivialise, but encourage them to feel what power they have in being able to use their thinking skills and their imagination.
- Do not go on for too long. Clients should neither be overwhelmed by the length of the list nor pressurised to come up with yet another possibility.

The final step is to appraise the list and discard options which are too costly in terms of time and energy or which require resources that the client may not have. For example, a client who wishes to change her job may not have the resources to do that immediately. She may need to retrain or update her existing skills before making applications.

3 *Sentence completion.* This is a simple way of encouraging clients to become more change orientated. It may be used in conjunction with the two preceding techniques. You simply ask clients to finish sentences. Consider the following example. A client, Felicity, has decided that she would like to be more sociable and less isolated. She has explored how she stops herself from entering relationships with others and now feels confident enough in herself to take the risk of seeking close friendships.

PRACTITIONER: Take your time and finish off the sentences I'll give you. I'll write down what you say and then we'll discuss it.
FELICITY: OK.
PRACTITIONER: This is the first sentence, 'If my social life were completely different to the way it is now, I would be . . .'

FELICITY: Well! [*smiles*] I'd be having a wonderful time. Yes. I'd be doing all sorts of exciting things with people I liked.

PRACTITIONER: What sort of things would you be doing?

FELICITY: Oh! Going to the theatre, sailing, learning to play the piano, brushing up my French. In fact, hearing myself say all of this, I don't know why I don't do these things now. They're not so out of the ordinary, are they?

Felicity and her practitioner review her statements and form a list of possible goals. For example, she decides that she will increase her theatre-going. However, the practitioner's hunch is that Felicity could go to the theatre on her own and not develop the friendships she says she wants.

PRACTITIONER: I'm not sure how this will put you in touch with others?

Felicity: I'm not sure either. It's something I'd like to do though; and I don't go to the theatre, because I don't have anyone to go with.

PRACTITIONER: I was wondering about theatre groups or evening classes that met for that purpose.

Felicity decides she will find out what evening classes or theatre groups there are in her area that would help to make theatre-going a more social occasion.

You might use questions that focus on different degrees of success. For example, you might ask clients to respond to:

'If I were coping with this issue a little better I would be . . .'

'If I were coping with this problem much better, I would be . . .'

So far in this section on goal setting, we have considered several techniques for helping clients *identify* options or goals. Before considering what might be involved in planning action to achieve one or more of them, clients need to be helped to *evaluate* them in order to be able to make an informed decision.

Helping clients to appraise goals and decide which to opt for, using force field analysis

Clients may favour some options over others and have greater chances of success with some than others. One valuable technique that has stood the test of time for appraising both goals and action plans is that of 'force field analysis' (Lewin, 1969). Let us look at what is involved.

Each of us occupies a 'life-space' that encompasses our physical surroundings, the community and family ties that we have, as well as aspects of ourselves as people – interests, values, strengths, achievements. People's life-spaces are bounded by their physical, emotional and cognitive horizons. One way of viewing a life-space is to see it as an arena in which the various 'forces' are competing. Some of the forces will be positive and will help clients towards their goals. Some will be negative and inhibit their success. If clients want to achieve change, one way of assessing the feasibility of any change or goal is to ascertain which things in their 'life-spaces' will be positive and help them to achieve what they want and which will inhibit their progress, or go against them. Perhaps the best way to illustrate the technique is to give a specific example.

Deirdre's goal is to obtain a full-time place on a degree course in Business Studies, starting in the next academic year. She has the required entry qualifications but is finding it hard to implement the decision. Her goal is clear, specific and within her resources. She lists all the things that would facilitate her achievement of that goal and all the things that would prevent or inhibit her. Thus:

Positives	Negatives
Fulfil an ambition	Partner is not supportive
Leave a boring job	Anxiety that I'll fail
Time for study and spouse	Less personal money
Some savings to supplement income	Job is secure and well paid
Skills which can get me part-time work	Life is settled
Friends supportive	Change is disruptive
Partner has a well paid job	
Use qualifications	
Determination	

When recording what clients say, use their words. Continue by exploring each positive and negative force. Ask clients to expand on and discuss the implications of each force. Some practitioners ask clients to rate statements or to rank them in order of importance. For example, Deirdre said that lack of support from her partner was the most inhibiting force on her list and the one that would be the most difficult to overcome.

You will need your exploration and challenging skills to help clients to appraise their lists. For example, Deirdre's practitioner asked her precisely what she meant when she said her partner was unsupportive. Is it another way of saying that he is highly concerned that she will change and decide to leave him? Reviewing her list, Deirdre may decide that the negatives far outweigh the positives and this goal is not for her. She can then move on and look at some other options, such as part-time training or distance learning.

Using force field analysis is an excellent way of encouraging clients to see themselves in context. It reminds both client and practitioner alike that we do not live in a vacuum and we are not omniscient. Family ties and obligations, social and community pressures may all operate either for or against us. It is not the length of the lists of positives and negatives that is important but the weight that clients attach to each force. You will sometimes need to challenge clients to reassess their lists and, for instance, explore whether or not a force is really so negative. Thus, when Deirdre says that change is disruptive, her practitioner might offer her the view that change can also be exciting, energising and stretching.

Force field analysis should be a collaborative process. You may also wish to introduce aspects of your own, which you think that clients are overlooking. For example, some clients may say that they do not have the determination to sustain change. You may choose to point out times when they seem to have shown 'grit' in the past and ask them what is different now. Exploration and challenging will encourage clients to look afresh at what they have identified and the weightings they have allocated.

Guidelines for using force field analysis

1 Brainstorm the facilitating forces – those that will help clients reach their goals.
2 Brainstorm the inhibiting forces – those that will prevent clients from reaching their goals.
3 Check that the positives and negatives are 'real' and not 'assumed'.
4 Review what clients can do to maximise the positive forces and minimise the negative forces.
5 Decide on the feasibility of the goal.

If clients are to succeed in achieving the change they want, they need to be committed to the options that they have chosen. Using force field analysis will help clients to assess goals for their chances of success.

We want to discuss briefly a couple of difficulties often encountered in goal setting.

The goal is too large

Clients may want to make substantial change in their lives and may know clearly what they want to achieve. However, viewed all at once, the change seems daunting. Breaking down a large goal into a series of smaller ones will give clients a clearer focus for action and help them to maintain their effort. Achieving a small goal can boost confidence and may provide clients with the impetus to sustain their commitment to change.

Clients may also need to prioritise which goals to attempt first. For example, a client who has never had a close romantic/sexual relationship may need to develop his social skills before he risks approaching others. He may be being unrealistic in thinking that creating opportunities for meeting others is all he needs to do. He may not have the appropriate social skills to engage with others whom he meets and he may become de-motivated by his lack of success at making new relationships.

Clients who do not want to set goals

Some clients, by the very act of recounting their concerns, will see clearly what they want to achieve and what they can do to achieve it. Other clients may be reluctant to commit themselves to change. If this occurs, you have several options:

1   Return to your contract and remind clients of what they said they wanted to achieve by working with you. You may need to renegotiate the contract.
2   Raise the issue and challenge clients to examine their resistance and reluctance to change.
3   Ask clients what benefits they are getting from working with you, if they are not changing in the ways that they have said they wanted. Obtaining help through talking may be expensive in terms of time, effort and sometimes money. Clients may need to consider what pay-offs they are getting from their investment.

Change can be both liberating and frightening and you will need to be sensitive to this. However, supporting and challenging clients while they decide on what they want to accomplish is different from colluding with clients while they engage in fruitless exploration or debate.

To summarise, goal setting is an excellent strategy for:

1   identifying and focusing on what clients want to achieve
2   helping clients to direct their attention and to mobilise their resources
3   acting as a restraint against premature action (although some clients may need to act in order to discover what they want).

In order to be viable, goals should meet several criteria. Goals should:

* be wanted by clients
* be within the clients' resources
* be clear and precise in defining what clients will accomplish
* indicate clearly what clients will be doing differently and what others will see them doing
* be set within a reasonable and specific period of time
* make a significant contribution to resolving or handling clients' concerns

Clients will be more likely to shape successful goals if they choose from a range of possible options. Three of the ways in which clients can be helped to generate goals are: imagining better futures; brainstorming; sentence completion.

Vague ideas for change need to be tailored to feasible goals. Force field analysis can be used to help clients assess the feasibility of the goals they have identified, and choose the options they will go for.

Goal setting requires continued exploration and challenging if clients are to develop realistic options. Before taking any action, clients should be clear about what it is they want to achieve and be committed to their goals.

Let us now consider taking action.

Action planning

Once clients have decided upon their goals, the next step is to consider what action they will take to achieve them. The first step is to help clients to identify as many options as possible. Again, brainstorming is a useful technique whereby you can collaborate in producing alternatives. Clients may fail to change because they remain trapped in their limited view of the options for action available to them.

Consider the following example.

Hannah sought help because, in her own words, she 'felt awful' about herself. Her self-esteem was low; she saw herself as an unattractive woman whom no one would want to approach. Her self-evaluation prevented her from being close to others and from taking opportunities that were presented both socially and at work. Hannah decided that one of the ways she could feel more confident about herself would be to lose some weight and become fitter. Her practitioner asked her how she would achieve her weight loss. She replied:

HANNAH: [*with a look of distaste*] I thought I'd go on the diet I read about in a magazine; or maybe join a slimming club. That's about it really

PRACTITIONER: Those are two options. Any others you can think of?

HANNAH: There's only one way to lose weight, isn't there? It's very simple, stop eating so much. [*with a hectoring tone*] More deprivation!

PRACTITIONER: It's very simple [*reflection*] and you don't do it – it means deprivation and also by the sound of your voice associated with rules or being lectured at.

HANNAH: Yes! those old rules again, isn't it? – 'do this, don't do that, be good'. I guess I've rebelled when it comes to food and just thought to hell with it – I'm not going to be governed by what I can and can't eat. So what do I need to do?

PRACTITIONER: We could start by listing all the ways of losing weight and toning yourself. You can be as creative as you like. Once we have a list, we can review it and decide which ones appeal to you.

Here is Hannah's original list:

– go to a health farm to get a good start
– join a slimming club
– have my jaw wired or my stomach stapled
– take slimming pills
– take exercise like swimming
– fast one day per week
– eat what I like but give up alcohol
– take up smoking
– monitor myself and only eat when I'm hungry.

Hannah reviewed her list and rejected wiring her jaw – that seemed invasive and severe. Fasting one day per week felt like extreme deprivation. Taking slimming pills was excluded as an option because they were not in keeping with her values. She decided against giving up alcohol because she drank very little, enjoyed it and the loss in abstaining would far outweigh any benefits from weight loss. She hesitated over taking up smoking and then challenged herself, deciding that she would be compromising her health and swapping one problem for two was a 'poor deal'. She felt negative about the possibility of a health farm or a slimming club, considering them places for those who 'couldn't cope on their own'. Her practitioner challenged her and pointed out that she was overlooking the potential benefits of the support that a club might provide.

Hannah eventually decided to try out a slimming club on grounds of cost and as a result of speaking to a colleague at work who had found a club that met at midday. She thought that going along with a colleague might make the experience more pleasurable and give her an added incentive. In the process of identifying possible action steps, her practitioner challenged Hannah to explore what being hungry meant to her. She also attended to Hannah's feelings and challenged her to explore them. Hannah had told her practitioner that she *knew* what she had to do to lose weight, yet it was Hannah's feelings about 'old rules', together with her denial of her body's needs that were inhibiting her.

The process of identifying and choosing suitable action plans demands that you continue to explore with and challenge clients. Some clients may avoid certain possibilities for action because of their largely untested beliefs. For example, they may fear rejection or what will happen if they succeed. Others may be responding to outdated 'shoulds' and 'oughts' that do not reflect their current reality.

It is generally useful to ask clients how they will stop themselves from taking action. Once clients become aware of how they stop themselves, it is harder for them to continue doing it. The way is then open to explore how they can halt their attempts at self-sabotage. For example, a client who says that he tells himself 'You'll fail. You're not good enough' can be helped, among other ways, to identify positive messages to substitute for negative ones.

There are various techniques for helping clients to choose what action out of the many possibilities to take. We have previously discussed force field analysis as a method for assessing goals: this technique can also be used to assess the probable success or failure of action plans. Balance sheets are useful for reviewing the costs/benefits and probability of success of any action. If clients are aware of obstacles, they will be in a better position either to find ways of overcoming them or to look at other options that will not meet the same degree of opposition.

What stops clients from succeeding?

1 *They do not have the skills.* It may be unwise to encourage a person who has been in one job for a long time to start going for interviews without first honing their skills. Such a client may need to take a short course in self-presentation or to practise their interview skills with you.

2 *There are risks involved.* These might be real or imagined. We have touched on this in the previous section and we think it is important that clients explore their fears and beliefs about possible risks. Some clients may discover that they need information; others may realise that the risks they imagine do not belong to this situation at all. Risks can also be graded from 'High to Low'.

3 *There are constraints involved.* Clients do have real constraints in their lives and it is important that these are recognised and explored. However, they may also imagine constraints or over-estimate their significance.

4 *The rewards are not perceived as great enough.* Part of the action planning process is to help clients identify and create a reward system for themselves. You will need to help clients to decide whether the pay-offs for taking risks are ample enough for them. It is often worth exploring pay-offs if a client is struggling to find the motivation to implement previously selected goals. The fear of change may weigh more heavily than the hoped for gains.

5 *Clients want a perfect action plan.* There is, of course, no such thing. All change carries some risks and no plan is fail-safe. Clients can be helped both to identify risks and to discover options for minimising them.

Consider the following example. A client, Lucy, is talking about her five-year-old daughter.

LUCY: I want to be absolutely sure that I'm doing the right thing. I don't want her to become a delinquent or a drop-out. The early years are important, aren't they?

PRACTITIONER: I admire your concern and I think you're telling me that you want certainty.

LUCY: I do . . . and that's not possible, is it? I want to do my best though.

PRACTITIONER: OK – let's talk through what action you think would be the most successful and what doing your best means.

6   *Fear of ending.* Clients may be ambivalent about achieving their goal because this means ending their relationship with you. Clients may fear that, when they have achieved their goals, they will lose a relationship where they have felt respected, valued and supported. This wish to avoid ending may be a powerful deterrent to succeeding and moving on. In such circumstances, it may be best to separate the tasks of achieving the goal or implementing a desired action from ending the relationship. Once the desired outcomes have been achieved, the task of achieving a constructive ending can be addressed – see later in this chapter.

Taking action

In order to take and to sustain action, clients might need to do the following:

1   *Identify a suitable reward system.* By 'suitable', we mean one that fits clients' values, is both adequate and realistic and does not undermine the action plan. For example, a client who wishes to control his drinking would not be advised to reward himself with a wine-tasting event!

Rewards help clients both to get started and to maintain the commitment. You may reward clients by noticing changes they make and by praising new and positive behaviour. Logs and diaries can be helpful as 'progress charts'. A record of achievement is often rewarding for clients when the going gets tough.

One client was encouraged to record all the positive comments she received each week. She found it much harder to dismiss herself as stupid when faced with a list of compliments.

2   *Establish a support system.* If you are the client's only support, then you will need to raise this as an issue. The support of friends, family and colleagues can be important for any client who wants to change. Support systems provide many of the following: positive feedback, practical help, and opportunities for sharing ideas and information. Support systems also decrease clients' sense of isolation and help to establish a sense of 'universality' (see Chapter 8). It is not uncommon for clients to feel anxious when trying out new behaviours; and possible

too, that they may experience a decrease in enthusiasm for sticking to their action plan. Exploring with clients both what and who can support them when they feel anxious or when they feel like giving up may help to sustain them. You may also want to discuss what support and encouragement they would like from you.

Evaluating action and sustaining change

The key question to raise with clients concerns the relationship between the original problem or issue and the action they are taking. You might ask, 'Is the problem being resolved by this action?' If it is, then you and the client may consider ending the work. If not, then you will need to explore what is happening for the client. Sometimes taking action helps clients to see that the problem that they brought masks another deeper issue. Futhermore, the goals that clients set may be insufficient and need to be reassessed. Finally, timing is often crucial to successful action. Clients sometimes fail to achieve what they want because they time their action inappropriately, for example, the client who tries to discuss his relationship with his partner when she is putting their children to bed.

Helping clients to secure their future by sustaining the changes they have made is generally a feature of the Ending Stage. There are a number of considerations important to sustaining change and avoiding relapses into old and unhelpful behaviour patterns. In addition to establishing a support system, you might help clients to:

1 *Identify situations in which they are most likely to revert to their old behaviours.* For example, it may be under stress at work or during weekends when they are on their own. If they can identify times, places or people with whom they are likely to compromise their new behaviour, they can avoid these situations when they are feeling vulnerable.

2 *Identify environments that support the 'old' behaviour and avoid them.* For example, a client who wishes to stop smoking may find it more difficult if she continues to socialise in pubs with her friends and where smoking has been an enjoyable accompaniment to drinking.

3 *Observe and learn emotional control.* Clients may feel anxious when they experience a challenge to their new behaviour. They may believe they will go out of control or that they will be embarrassed. If clients can learn to identify their feelings (and the beliefs which accompany them), they will be in a position to control them and remain 'in charge'.

Consider the following example. Alice sought help because at times she behaved ineffectually at work. She described herself as 'powerless' and 'losing all her social skills'. In the Beginning and Middle Stages, Alice learned that her powerlessness was a defence against possible attack. She feared criticism because it was redolent of the disgrace she experienced as a child. Alice set goals to become more assertive and to control her fear. She explored what would happen if she faced criticism after she had expressed her views.

ALICE: Sometimes I'm aware of feeling very scared. I have an urge to withdraw and to protect myself. When I feel this way I say to myself, 'Stop and listen to others. You are competent and they can't destroy you. It's all right for people to disagree with you and that doesn't make you wrong or stupid.' That helps me to see what is *really* going on, rather than what I create.

4   *Create a system of internal rewards.* Self-praise coupled with knowledge of results can be powerful in helping clients to sustain their new behaviour. Recording, for example, their assertiveness, weight loss, abstinence from alcohol or cigarettes can provide a rewarding feedback system. If clients are hesitant to do this, ask them to keep a record for a trial period of two weeks.

Ending

Endings are an important part of the process and may be concerned with loss as well as with celebration of achievements. Let us consider some of the issues in ending.

When to end?

Using counselling skills in a contractual relationship provides opportunities to explicitly point out when clients have achieved what they set out to achieve or when they are coping sufficiently well with their concerns to need no further assistance. This chance for actively creating a positive ending may be more difficult to achieve in casual and opportunistic uses of counselling skills. For example, a client in a contractual counselling relationship in which she became accustomed to discussing what she wanted and her progress towards her goals remarked to her practitioner:

I feel much happier about saying what I think to my partner and I know I'm using my skills at work to be more direct with colleagues. I'm also aware that I could be more direct with my boss. I'm not handling that as well as I'd like but I'm satisfied with what I've achieved. So, I think I'll finish now.

Planning to end

One of the distinguishing characteristics of the contracted helping relationship is its temporary nature. From the outset, all the work that clients undertake moves them towards the time when they will no longer have the need or wish for support of this kind. You may need to remind clients of the number of contracted sessions you have left. . You might say something like: 'I'm aware that we have this and one further session of the six we originally contracted for. I'd like us to review how far you've got towards achieving what you wanted and to discuss options for further sessions, if you want them.'

You will need to plan your ending. The end will usually be signalled by clients achieving what they wanted. However, you will need to leave adequate time for them to identify, explore and express their feelings about the ending and the loss of the relationship. Clients will have spent time in your company revealing more of their secret fears and hopes than possibly at any previous time in their lives. You will have 'contained' them when they have expressed intense feelings and been witness to the side of themselves that they have found unacceptable. The ending of the helping relationship may resonate with other painful endings that they have experienced and perhaps never resolved.

Consider the following example. Ken is a male student who has been supported by his pastoral tutor throughout his course that is now close to completion.

TUTOR: Next week will be our last session and I was wondering how you feel
   about that?
KEN: Not much really. [*looking at his feet*] If it's ending, that's it, isn't it?
TUTOR: [*playing a hunch*] I wonder what usually happens in endings in your
   life?
KEN: [*looking bright*] Nothing, because I avoid them!
TUTOR: I shall miss seeing you.
KEN: [*in tears*] This is why I avoid them. I get sad.

The tutor encouraged Ken to express his sadness. They explored the ending of their relationship. Ken made a connection between dismissing the importance of the ending and his initial contract with his tutor. At the start of the relationship he had a poor self-image and low self-esteem. His wish to avoid focusing on the ending had to do with his old belief that he was too insignificant to be missed and he had therefore decided not to miss others.

Alerting clients to the possibility of feelings of sadness and loss

Clients may not expect to experience painful feelings at the ending of their relationship with you. However, alerting them to the possibility can be a way both of giving them permission and of preparing them for what may occur. We are not suggesting that clients *ought* to feel sad and that something is amiss if they do not; rather that some clients, particularly those who have difficulty expressing feelings, may feel freer to articulate what feelings they do have, if the issue is raised with them. You might say something like:

> PRACTITIONER: I'm aware that we haven't talked about how you're feeling.
> CLIENT: I feel OK. It seems the right thing to do. I'm much more confident now; and I'm developing new friendships and life seems much freer.
> PRACTITIONER: You sound much stronger. I also wondered if there was any sadness for you in this ending?
> CLIENT: I'm not aware of feeling sad, [*pause*] although it will seem really strange not coming here any more.

Being open to negative feelings

Not all relationships end when clients have completed the work of their contracts. Some clients will end the relationship prematurely in your view, because they believe you are not helping them. It is not possible to help every client who walks through the door and some will resist your efforts, no matter how skilful you are being. Practitioners also make mistakes. You can but do your best with the skills and knowledge that you have and ensure that you have good supervision to support your work. However, it is sometimes hard to receive negative feedback from clients about their experience of seeking help from you. The following may assist you at such times:

Guidelines for handling negative feedback

1   Offer to support clients in their search for another practitioner. It may be that they would benefit from working with someone else, who has a different style and approach.
2   Use your reflective skills to accept their disappointment or anger.
3   Give feedback about how you feel in a non-judgemental way.
4   Describe concretely what you think has happened and own your part in it. However, we do not mean that you take responsibility for clients' failure to commit themselves to change.
5   Respect clients' right to do what they want to do. You may think that they have more work to do and would not advise finishing at this juncture. However, they have the right to look elsewhere and to decide what is best for them.
6   If appropriate, review what you think have been the positive steps they have taken in their work with you.

Review the learning

Endings provide an opportunity for clients to appraise their learning and development, and to update their views of themselves. Encourage participation; reviews are neither tests nor processes that are 'done to' clients. Dryden (1989) has suggested the following guidelines for helping clients both to focus and to reflect on the work they have done with you.

Guidelines (Dryden, 1989)

1   Ask clients to think back to how they were at the start of your work together and to compare what they are doing differently now. Relate their new behaviours to the contracts they made with you and encourage them to take credit for their achievements. Share your perception of how they have changed. Make sure that the feedback you give is specific and focused.
2   If you have taped your work you might want to play a piece of tape that demonstrates clients' new thinking or their new insights.
3   Share and discuss what have been the critical or important times in your work together.
4   Look to the future and spend some time discussing how clients will use their new behaviour to tackle other related issues or anticipated problems.

The review provides opportunities for positive feelings associated with appraising the history of the work undertaken together, the achievements accomplished and hopes for a better future. A good ending will acknowledge what is being lost as well as celebrating what has been accomplished in ways that will enrich the future lives of both people.

Summary

The Ending Stage typically has action and closure as its foci.

Goals are developed from the new insights gained through the process of challenging. They are 'what' clients wish to achieve; in other words, the outcomes they value and regard as important for coping with their concerns. Goals are the opposite of problems.

To be viable, goals should be within clients' resources and specify clearly what the outcome will be.

Action plans are based on the goals that the client has chosen. They identify precisely how clients will achieve their goals.

Ending the relationship will usually occur when clients have achieved their stated goals. Consideration needs to be given to the end of the relationship and the significance of that for clients.

7

CASE STUDY
Bereavement

All the case examples presented so far have been used to illustrate specific aspects of this integrative approach to using counselling skills. In this chapter, we propose to demonstrate how work with a client moves between the stages. We want to capture some of the difficulties and challenges faced by anyone who is attempting to use this structure. In real life, helping does not typically conform to the neat and linear progression of theoretical models. There are frequent instances where the practitioner has to review which strategies and skills would be appropriate. We also want to illustrate how an understanding of the issue presented by the client can inform and suggest the use of specific strategies and skills.

The example we have chosen is of a client being supported through grieving. An inescapable part of life, bereavement is a powerful and potentially deeply painful and disturbing experience. Counselling can provide the kind of emotional and practical support that not only helps the bereaved through the mourning, but also diminishes the increased risk of illness or morbidity and mortality that follows any significant bereavement. (Woof and Carter, 1997a, 1997b).

The case study is fictitious but draws upon different aspects of our experience – as practitioners and trainers. It is intended to be a realistic account of how counselling skills can be used effectively in different roles. We certainly believe that no one, especially someone who is newly trained, should provide services that use counselling skills without adequate personal and professional support. So we have included examples of how good support can enhance the help that is offered to clients.

Background of the practitioner

Aneena started training in counselling skills out of a desire to be more helpful to a longstanding friend who had been diagnosed as being in the early stages of a progressive and ultimately terminal illness. The training has been more useful than she expected. She has learnt a great deal about herself and how she relates to others. This experience has helped her to be more supportive of her friend while still meeting some of her own needs. She believes that the friendship between them has deepened and yet become more fun, at least on the good days. Inspired by these positive experiences, she has considered the possibility of using her training in counselling skills as a way of opening up new career opportunities. Aneena feels stale and under-used at work where she is a team leader in a large administrative section. She is wondering whether to apply to mentor trainees or to become a member of the staff welfare team. Both options are possible ways of developing her career.

Responding to the Unexpected

As Aneena walks into her workplace on Monday morning, she decides to suspend her thoughts about her future career options and concentrate on preparing for an impending quality audit. On entering her section, she notices that one of the new members of staff has returned from a few days' sickness leave. Everyone, including Aneena, assumed that Pat's absence was due to the feverish cold that had been going around the office. Aneena is glad to see her back, as she is the person responsible for organising the files to be inspected later that week. Pat is the sort of person who would clear any work rapidly. Some of her colleagues find her overconfident and bossy but Aneena thinks that Pat's organising skills will be an asset to the overall team performance.

Aneena notices that Pat seems unusually withdrawn but thinks no more about it. No doubt she will find out more when Pat hands in her sick certificate. She hopes that Pat has not returned before she has fully recovered. She puts these thoughts to the back of her mind as she allocates tasks for the day and does some preparation for a meeting later that morning. She has just returned from her meeting when there is a knock at the door. Pat comes in holding her certificate and stands there looking uncharacteristically helpless and distracted. Pat speaks softly and hesitantly.

PAT: I don't know what to put down as my reason for being off on this self-certification form. [*She holds out the blank certificate.*]

ANEENA: I think that most people have put down viral infection or heavy cold.

PAT: [*hesitantly*] I . . . could do that . . . but it wouldn't really be . . . true.

ANEENA: [*Lifting her head and becoming more attentive*] I see. Come in and sit down . . . [*As Pat sits down, Aneena moves from behind her desk and sits opposite her.*] You sound worried, tell me what's been happening. [*paraphrase and directive*]

PAT: [*looking sad and awkward*] I'm worried that you'll think I've been irresponsible and let you down over the audit. I just couldn't come to work. It was so sudden and unexpected. One day he was there and the next he is gone, without any warning.

ANEENA: Someone's left you and that's shocked and upset you. [*paraphrase that links an event with the stated feelings – basic empathy*]

PAT: Yes I am. It's worse than that. He was rushing out of the house to go on a site visit. I was really cross with him because he was leaving the kitchen in a mess. He *never* clears up after himself. I swore at him as he went out. He slammed the door. That's the last I saw him. He was killed in the pile-up on the motorway later that day . . . crushed between two lorries. I thought he was still narked with me for shouting at him, when he didn't come home at his usual time. When the police knocked at the door, I just knew something terrible had happened to . . . [*Pat tails off because she is crying.*]

ANEENA: [*Shocked and wondering who the man was and what he meant to Pat, Aneena hesitates. She stifled her curiosity and concentrated on Pat's anguish. She leaned forward.*] You've had a dreadful shock – no wonder you didn't want to face coming in to work. [*paraphrase to focus on content and feelings – more basic empathy using the disclosed feelings*]

PAT: Yes, and I had no idea that he means so much to me. We just shared the flat for companionship after John and I split up. It suited us. Peter is an old friend. He's really good fun and makes me laugh when I'm feeling down. There were lots of low moments after John left me for that other woman.

ANEENA: Peter is important to you – a good friend to you when you were alone. [*restating and following the client's lead in talking as though he is still alive*]

PAT: I can't believe he's gone and won't come back. It's just too sudden . . . too terrible to believe. It is so unfair. He is such a kind man. He doesn't deserve to be taken away like that . . . [*sobs uncontrollably*]

ANEENA: [*passes Pat some tissues and sits quietly and attentively until she stops crying*] [*respectfully affirms client's grief and offers practical support*]

PAT: [*calmer*] Sorry. I hadn't meant to get so upset. I've been feeling terrible since it happened and haven't cried 'til now . . . I haven't spoken to anyone for days, it must just have been building up. I wanted to get back to work just to have some company and to get into a routine again.

ANEENA: I was wondering whether it's too soon to come back to work. You're saying that you think coming to work will help you. [*self-disclosure and paraphrase*]

PAT: [*briskly*] Yes. I wasn't sure but it has helped talking to you. I always feel better when I have company and something practical to do. From what I know about the state of those files I'll have plenty to do.

ANEENA: It sounds as if you've made up your mind. You know what will help you. Come and talk to me again if you find that it's all getting too much. If you're agreeable, I'll discuss what to put on your sick note with personnel.

PAT: [*relieved*] Thanks Aneena. That would be really helpful. I don't want to explain all this again today.

ANEENA: You said, talking to me has helped. I wonder if talking to our staff counsellor would also help. It's completely confidential and I can arrange for you to see him in work time. [*paraphrases to check and gives information*]

PAT: Can I think about it? I don't mind when I see him but it sounds like a good idea. Thank you. I'm feeling much better than when I came in.

A few days later, Pat is sitting in the counsellor's office. Brian has been the staff counsellor for several years and is accredited as a practitioner by the British Association for Counselling and Psychotherapy. He originally trained as a person-centred counsellor and remains committed to that approach. More recently, he has become interested in short-term and brief counselling because of the need to adapt to the time-constraints of providing a service in the workplace. He tries to avoid using technical language or counselling jargon. When he is asked how he works he describes his approach as taking his lead from the client and paying particular attention to the quality of the relationship that develops. He believes that these are the essential elements of successful counselling.

Just before Pat arrives for her first session, Brian's secretary tells him that Pat seemed hesitant about coming to see him. After making the appointment, she phoned to cancel and 15 minutes later reinstated the appointment. Brian has decided that this might be a sufficiently important issue to discuss during the opening phase, even though he wants to be careful not to take control and impose his own agenda. After he has greeted Pat and they are both sitting down, he begins.

Session 1

BRIAN: Pat, I'm aware that you cancelled and then reinstated this appointment. I was wondering if you have some concerns about coming here and whether it would be helpful to discuss them. [*statements to focus and encourage*]

PAT: You're right, I very nearly didn't come. Last time I talked about it, I got very upset. I felt embarrassed to be so upset at work. I'm also worried about people in my office knowing what's happening.

BRIAN: Whatever you tell me is confidential. My secretary also safeguards the confidentiality of anyone using this service. The only time I might consider breaking confidentiality is if I believe that you are a serious risk to yourself or others, especially to the other employees. I would normally discuss this with you first before doing anything. You also mentioned being embarrassed and I understand that being upset can feel awkward. We are used to it here. I have ten minutes between appointments so that, if you want to, you can sit here quietly or use the cloakroom next door before going back to work. Is anything else concerning you? [*summarises key information and paraphrases, closed question to check*]

PAT: [*hesitantly and looking uncomfortable*] I suppose that I'm a bit afraid . . . that you might tell me that I'm mad.

BRIAN: I might tell you that you're mad . . . *and* that scares you.' [*reflection linked to a disclosed feeling – basic empathy – inviting further disclosure*]

PAT: It's not that. It's just that . . . [*voice fading*]

BRIAN: Something else? [*question to prompt*]

PAT: Yes, I suppose I feel safer at work. I'm not sure that I want to look at what is troubling me here. I can forget myself in my work.

BRIAN: You can escape what is worrying you. [*paraphrase*]

PAT: Yes. There's a lot to do, getting files ready for an audit, so I don't have time to think . . . [*long pause*] Also, he doesn't speak to me here.

BRIAN: You don't hear him here. [*paraphrase to check and focus on what has been difficult to say*]

PAT: [*looking uncomfortable*] Oh dear. I was afraid that this might happen and

it would come out. That's why I didn't want to come. I don't want you to
think that I'm mad or have to be stopped from working. How can
someone who is hearing voices look after important files?

BRIAN: You're afraid that you're going mad because you hear voices and you
also said that 'He doesn't speak to me at work.' [*paraphrases and uses
a statement to probe further*]

PAT: [*leaning forward and with some energy*] It's just the one voice. We are
such good friends. I hear him saying, 'Put your best foot forward.
Waggle those hips and don't worry.' And then I hear him chuckle.
Sometimes he says I will be all right and teases me that he will be
keeping an eye on me. The uncanny thing is that sometimes I think that
I can see him in the distance or out of the corner of my eye. Sometimes
I can smell him. It feels strange, but it's not as frightening as it sounds.

BRIAN: So you're not afraid of hearing your friend's voice or feeling him close
to you. Sounds like it might be comforting in some way. [*paraphrases
and offers a possible reframing of her concern*]

PAT: Yes. In a strange way it helps. I feel as though he is still here, just around
the next corner. It's as though it never happened.

BRIAN: Something upsetting has happened. Something that means he can't
be with you but you are reassured by hearing his voice and feeling him
close to you. [*longer paraphrase to summarise*]

PAT: That's it . . .

Brian has a hunch that someone close to Pat has died, and chooses not to
share it. He wants to allow Pat to tell her story in her own way.

Pat explains about Peter's sudden death. She had known him since she
was 17 years old and had hoped that they would become more than friends.
She realised that she wanted Peter to become something 'that was not
really him'. He had said that if there was any woman that he wanted to
'sweep off her feet and marry, it would be her', but that he was more
attracted to men.

Later she had married John who had tolerated rather than liked Peter.
One of the few positive outcomes from John leaving her was having the
opportunity to revive her friendship with Peter. They were both recover-
ing from the break-up of relationships. Their friendship had deepened.
Peter often stayed with her when he was working in the area.

PAT: He is my best friend, the person who probably knows me best. I so wish
now that my last words to him hadn't been complaining about the mess

he had left in the kitchen. He slammed the door on his way out and I
don't know whether he was angry or just in a hurry. Somehow hearing
his voice is reassuring, telling me that maybe it doesn't matter.

BRIAN: That maybe you don't have to reproach yourself for being angry with
him. [*paraphrase to encourage*]

PAT: And that it wouldn't matter, we'll always be friends.

BRIAN: When we started you were afraid to tell me that you heard Peter's
voice because it might mean that I'd think that you were mad and that
you shouldn't be at work. Instead I hear you saying that it consoles you
and gives you a sense of your friendship with Peter. [*paraphrase to
challenge*]

PAT: That's right. I did feel nervous – that you might think I was going mad
because I hear the voice of a dead person! I feel very different now . . .
less scary. It's kind of a relief.

Brian considers this brief response to indicate that they may have moved
beyond the Beginning Stage of exploration. Pat is reporting that her feelings have changed during the session, and the brevity of the response
indicates that she no longer feels the need to give further information.
Brian is mindful of how alone she sounded in her fear of going mad and
decides that this may be the time to offer some information. He suspects
that, if he had offered it earlier, Pat would probably have heard it as false
reassurance. Now that she has disclosed some of her concerns, Brian hopes
that she may be able to trust it as a supportive and carefully considered
response to her situation. He is aware that giving information is a challenge
and likely to be more effective in the Middle Stage.

BRIAN: There is nothing you have told me so far that is causing me to worry
about your sanity. I have heard other people talk about hearing the
deceased person's voice in the days following their death. I had a similar
experience when a close colleague died of a heart attack. It's not much
talked about. It's a common experience and you are not alone with it.
I'm glad that you find what Peter says reassuring. [*uses carefully timed
reassurance in the form of relevant information; also self-discloses to
reinforce the reassurance*]

PAT: I am such a practical and down-to-earth sort of person. I was
worried that I was losing my grip and going mad. It's a relief to
know that you have experienced it. You've come through it all right
yourself then?

BRIAN: [*Resisting the temptation to say too much about his own loss of a friend and colleague, he searches for a way of answering her question that keeps the focus of attention on Pat*] Yes. I think so. I'll always miss him but I am through the worst of grieving for him. I can think how glad I am that I knew him. I found counselling a support and wonder whether you think that it will be useful for you. [*uses self disclosure to encourage and reassure Pat*]

PAT: It helps to know that others have been through something similar and survived.

BRIAN: I hoped that it would. We've got about ten minutes left now and before we consider whether to meet again I want to check out something you said earlier. You were anxious about the prospect of having counselling here at work. You suggested that work is a safe place, where you can stop thinking about Peter's death. I wondered if talking here has somehow spoiled your sense of having somewhere to escape to. I can put you in touch with someone who would see you outside work.

PAT: That is what I *did* think. Or at least that is what I thought when we started. Now I think that I was more concerned about getting upset and not letting someone at work know about hearing Peter's voice. I don't hear him here, only in places where we would usually be together. I can keep myself busy here and for a while everything seems back to normal until I think about going home. I would like to see you again and see if you can help me. I don't want to have to tell it all again. Just like when I talked to Aneena, who suggested that I came here. I feel better now, but I don't know how long it will last.

They make an appointment to see each other again in a week. Pat takes a few minutes to adjust her make-up in the cloakroom and leaves to return directly to work. Before seeing his next client, Brian takes a few moments to review his impressions and sketch a plan of how he might continue working with Pat.

Brian notes his initial impressions:

- Early stages of bereavement following an unexpected death of close friend, Peter.
- Possibly complicated by unresolved losses following separation from husband – watch for this.
- Worried about hearing Peter's voice and sensing his presence – also comforted by what is said – watch to see if this becomes less frequent.

- Some clues that Pat has a sense of what she valued in the relationship as well as what irritated her, which may augur well for later in the grieving process – seems to be a realistic view of her friend rather than a history of ambivalent feelings that could complicate the grieving – may need to watch for this.
- During the initial session I have stayed mostly with beginning stage strategy and skills – noted that I had to resist a desire to talk about Peter in the past as I reflected Pat's statements that often suggested his on-going presence – reality of death still not fully appreciated – typical of early stages of grieving especially following sudden death – watch for movement towards talking about Peter in the past tense.
- No religious or cultural points of reference – this suggests Pat views bereavement in secular terms as primarily a personal process – may need to check this later.

Brian realises that he has many potential developments to consider. This is not unusual in the early stages of a counselling relationship. He finds that noting possibilities and issues to 'watch for' helps him both to remain open to his client's experience and to monitor subsequent developments. He decides that Pat is sufficiently vulnerable to justify discussing her in supervision. These discussions are undertaken anonymously in ways that protect Pat's identity so as to be respectful of her entitlement to confidentiality. The session had been very full with many potential issues for subsequent meetings. Brian wants to make sure that he is not missing something.

Counselling Supervision

Counselling supervision is a form of confidential consultation. Sometimes referred to as 'non-managerial' supervision, it is typically undertaken with someone who does not have line responsibility for the work with the client. Supervision essentially provides opportunities for maintaining and enhancing the quality of service that the practitioner provides by offering personal support to the practitioner in what could otherwise be a very isolated and potentially stressful role.

Mindful that this first session was an initial assessment, Brian presents his impressions and reviews his client under his usual headings, a framework of Work, Relationships and Identity (see Chapter 4):

Work

Pat values her work. She has a sense of what she can offer and appears to relish the challenge of preparing files for audit. At the moment work is a refuge from difficult feelings associated with the loss. This is probably healthy but needs to be watched so that it isn't a retreat to workaholism to escape grieving or to fill a social void in her life. No other goals or interests referred to.

Relationships

● *With others*

Pat may be socially isolated after moving here following separation from her husband. No close relationships referred to other than the deceased. Ambiguous whether these are eclipsed by a sudden death or do not exist.

● *With the counsellor*

Pat seems to be able to form a trusting relationship in which she can voice difficult feelings and experiences directly without denial or exaggeration.

Identity

Pat has a strong sense of being down-to-earth and practical. She seems able to voice her opinions and values directly and non-defensively. She seems to value her own resourcefulness. She might well want to develop herself further in the future. Despite her grieving, she has energy and a sense of purpose.

The supervisor, Rachel, checks how Brian will distinguish between the usual auditory and other sensory manifestations of the presence of someone who has recently died and psychosis. In a typical bereavement the voices and visions tend to occur less frequently and cease after a while. In psychosis, not only does the sense of the other person persist but it may become more intense and intrusive. Rachel and Brian do some preliminary planning about the possibility of a complex grief reaction. Brian would usually only offer six sessions, but it is agreed that it would be wise to offer open-ended counselling in this case as it takes time for complex grief reactions to emerge. Multiple losses, in this case separation and bereavement, and possible ambivalence towards the deceased person indicate an increased risk of complex grief reactions. Brian considers Pat to be self-reliant and unlikely to want to extend counselling beyond its usefulness.

Rachel turns the discussion to Brian. She is aware that about a year ago, he lost a close friend and colleague. She is interested in whether he might be seeking to reaffirm his own experience through Pat or listening to the quality and nature of her experience. Rachel provides Brian with the opportunity to explore his feelings over the sudden death of his friend and colleague and to reflect on how Pat's experience might resonate. Her aim is to support Brain's work by helping him to use his own experiences, with the awareness that they are separate and distinct from Pat's.

Session 2

Pat looks tired, sad and is more irritable. She has thrown herself into work and worked during both evenings and the previous weekend to prepare for the audit that has now taken place. She has been complimented on the quality of her work. The outcome of the audit has been successful. Brian uses beginning strategies and skills as Pat recounts her achievements. He is uncertain whether to stay with Beginning Stage interventions or to become more challenging. He opts for the latter.

BRIAN: You've been telling me about your well-deserved success. You're pleased that the auditors have singled you out for special comment. How positive Aneena has been. I can't help but notice the contrast between your success and how sad and tired you look. [*paraphrases and gives feedback*]

PAT: [*speaking crossly*] Just listen to you! Peter would have known how to celebrate. We would have been cracking the champagne and planning the next challenge.

BRIAN: [*gently*] You're angry that I'm not like Peter and you don't have him to celebrate with. [*paraphrases to acknowledge feeling*]

PAT: Yes . . . No... I don't know. I really miss him. I don't even hear his voice now. It's like he is fading away. A few weeks ago I would have been so proud to have achieved this. [*crying*] Now it feels pointless and empty.

BRIAN: Even success tastes bitter without Peter. [*empathic paraphrase to acknowledge the core feeling*]

PAT: It's worse than that. I don't like who I have become. I'm becoming a bad-tempered old witch who curses other people's happiness. I get cross at the slightest thing. John phoned me to see if I was all right. Instead of being grateful for his concern I reminded him that he didn't like Peter – called him a homophobic bastard or worse. I even threw in his face that, if he really cared for me, he wouldn't have left me for that tart he is with now. I could tell that he was really shaken. I have never spoken to anyone as ferociously as that before. We had tried to part on friendly terms . . . but I just felt this rage take over.

BRIAN: Your anger and hurt at being abandoned by two men you have loved just kicked in and you let rip at the survivor. [*paraphrase to clarify the source of her rage*]

PAT: I guess so . . . I felt like I had no control and my anger just took over. I had no idea that I felt so strongly . . . [*momentarily smiling and speaking ruefully*] Neither had John.

After a few more reflections in response to Pat describing other situations where she has been uncharacteristically angry, Brian explains that sadness and anger are often closely related. The rawness of her anger tells them both a lot about the depth of her grief.

PAT: [*looking relieved and reflective*] That's about it . . . I really do miss Peter. He's been the best friend I'll ever have. I suppose I'm angry with him for dying, and frustrated because I don't want to walk away from him and just forget him, but I don't want to go on feeling this sore and sad for much longer.

BRIAN: From everything you've said about him, I don't think that Peter would want you to feel so grief-stricken either. [*paraphrase to confirm and offer support from earlier disclosures that there is no pressure on her to prolong the intensity of her grief*]

PAT: Absolutely not! He was definitely one for living life to the full and enjoying what you've got. I think that he would be encouraging me to use my success and look for a more challenging job. I'm lucky, because so many women I know seem to be surrounded by men who encourage them to settle for less than they can achieve.

BRIAN: I'm getting a real sense of just how important Peter was to you. We've got about five minutes left before we finish this session. I wonder what it has meant for you? [*immediacy that affirms the client's experience, an early warning of the imminent end of the session, and a question designed to draw the session to a close and obtain feedback on how the session has been experienced*]

PAT: I think I understand where my anger is coming from now. I am shocked at
the energy it releases compared to how low I feel when I'm sad. I don't
feel like I've developed a split personality quite as much as before we
started talking. I can see now that they are two sides of my grief for Peter
and perhaps for what happened between John and me . . . There is one
thing that we haven't had time to consider. Now that my job is back to
normal, there isn't enough in it for me. I wonder about moving on.

BRIAN: This is something we can look at next time. Most counsellors would
recommend avoiding making life-changes immediately following
bereavement because grief travels with you and you are leaving familiar
supports behind you. It can complicate or delay getting through the
grief. We can look at whether this general guidance might apply to you
next time. [*gives information that is immediately helpful and may form
part of the agenda for the next session*]

As Brian reviews the session he experiences mixed reactions. He senses that
Pat is moving gradually towards accepting the reality of Peter's death with
the sorrow and rage that often accompanies an emerging sense of the
reality of the loss. Her fears of madness have disappeared with the gradual
loss of a sense of Peter's presence. Brian feels moved by her sense of
sadness and admires the way she was able to express her feelings. He is still
uncertain about the relationship between any unresolved grief over the
break-up of Pat's marriage and Peter's death. The significance of work and
friends in her life remains unresolved and still needs 'to be watched'. He is
aware that it is still early days and that a great deal could yet emerge.

Session 3

Pat starts the session undecided about whether to talk about a disagreement she has had with Aneena about attending Peter's funeral, or the
possibility of moving jobs.

BRIAN: I am wondering whether this has anything to do with our last session
when you felt reluctant to consider life without Peter but equally you
didn't want to remain feeling so sad. [*linking paraphrase to affirm and
offer the theme of ambivalence*]

PAT: Not at all. I do still feel that . . . but this is different. It's about something
that has happened since we last met. I can't decide what to talk about.

I've had an argument with Aneena. She thinks that I should have gone to Peter's funeral. She was willing to give me time off but I didn't want to go. She got annoyed and I snapped back. I'm not sure how it happened and I want to know what to say to her. On the other hand, all that might be history and irrelevant if I decide to change jobs, which is what we thought we might look at last time. Aneena and I haven't said much to each other since and it's 'nagging' at me.

BRIAN: I can see that there might not be time for both issues today and that both matter to you. We need to decide where to start.

PAT: Yes. I suppose so – but how?

BRIAN: Well! You say the disagreement is 'nagging' at you with some power in your voice. That seems to be uppermost in your mind. It suggests that this could be a promising place to start. [*offers a figure–ground perspective*] [*pauses for thought and notices that Pat is hesitant*] Perhaps before you make a decision we should consider how you are going to make a choice. On what basis will you decide between them? For example, will it be because one of them is causing you more distress now compared to the other? Which issue, if we tackled it now, would have the most positive influence on your life?

PAT: Yes – the 'spat' with Aneena is upsetting me, but the decision about whether I change jobs is a big decision and will have the biggest influence on my life. It's where I spend most of my waking hours and most of my energy. I know Peter would encourage me to act positively. He would say, 'Use success like a surfer. Ride the crest of the wave.' He'd encourage me to get going while the success is still fresh.

BRIAN: Whether to change jobs that would have the biggest impact on your life and you would also be following Peter's encouragement. [*paraphrase to acknowledge the importance of what has been said*]

PAT: Yes. And Peter isn't here any more. He always was very pushy. I think that's why he was so successful, but I'm different. People matter to me. Aneena has been a great help and she is still here. I think that, if I left now, I would feel that I was letting her down and running away from something I don't understand. Perhaps if I sort out what has happened between us, I will be better placed to decide about changing work.

BRIAN: So understanding what happened with Aneena will help you with the bigger decision. [*paraphrase to clarify*]

PAT: It is also closer to the pain I feel.

BRIAN: So it's tied to where you experience the greatest distress. [*paraphrase to empathise*]

PAT: Yes. Because it involves both Peter and Aneena. The argument was with Aneena but it was about Peter's funeral.

BRIAN: It sounds as though you've identified what's concerning you most. Shall we concentrate on that for now?

Pat agrees and goes on to explore her puzzlement and hurt that someone who has usually understood her so well seems to be adding to her sense of pain. She is clear she did not want to go Peter's funeral which was largely a family affair. She does want to be involved in the memorial service which will involve Peter's friends. She knows that Peter's family struggled to accept his gayness and concealed it from some of the extended family. She imagined that they will be grieving over both the loss of Peter and any future possibility of grandchildren from their only son.

She knew that Peter had been very hurt by their difficulty in accepting him as he was. It was one of the reasons why he was so determined to be a success, in order to gain their approval. Not attending his funeral meant that she would avoid having to choose between being 'true to Peter' and respecting his family's grief. Pat has been really clear about this in her own mind until Aneena had said that she might regret not going to the funeral for the rest of her life. Aneena had been quite emotional when she had said this. Brian encouraged Pat to consider the possible reasons for Aneena being so emotional. For a while Pat was puzzled until she remembered that Aneena had told her that one of her closest friends was suffering from a long-standing illness that was likely to be fatal in the next year or so. It was something that Aneena had told her shortly after she started working for her and something that Pat had completely forgotten, until now. Suddenly Pat could see that Aneena was really talking about herself and how she hoped she would be able to cope with the death of her friend, rather than understanding Pat's situation. This was so unlike Aneena. Pat sensed the depth of Aneena's pain and began to appreciate how they were both struggling with dying friends, albeit in very different circumstances. Her annoyance with Aneena softened and she began to feel concern for her. She had felt silenced by the strength of Aneena's opinion but now she wanted to talk to Aneena and discuss why she felt so strongly. She also knew that Aneena was the first generation of her Asian family to be born and brought up in Britain. Pat started to wonder whether there was a cultural or religious significance in not attending funerals. She realised that she knew very little about this aspect of Aneena's life. The session ended with her deciding to find an opportune time to discuss this with Aneena.

Session 4

The session opens with Pat reporting her discussion with Aneena. They have talked and cried together over each other's sense of loss. Pat has also learned something of the pain experienced by families living abroad because of the impossibility of attending funerals where the tradition is to hold the ceremonies within twenty-four hours after death. This talk has been a very positive experience for Pat. However, Pat says that a few days later she was again irritable with Aneena. They had snapped at each other about a file that had gone missing in Aneena's office. Pat looks distraught as she recounts the argument – especially when she recalls saying, 'At least your friend is still alive. Peter is dead.'

> PAT: I don't know where all this anger comes from. I have always been a little fiery but never like this before. I feel so alone without Peter. In the evenings I keep looking at his empty chair. I haven't even put away his toothbrush and razor in the bathroom. Part of me is still hoping that he will come back and everything will be how it used to be. I want Peter back. I want my old self back; I want things to be as they were.
>
> BRIAN: Of course you do and you're not ready to let him go and move on. [*paraphrase that affirms the intensity of her feelings*]
>
> PAT: [*angrily*] No! I am not. You say some silly things. It's not much of a job is it, just sitting there and repeating what I say. What good does that do?
>
> BRIAN: You're angry with me because I pointed to your sense of loss and I can't take your misery away.
>
> PAT: Too damn right I am! . . . You're useless! [*After a pause and much quieter*] There I go again. I have this rage that just takes over. The words shoot out before I know what they will be.
>
> BRIAN: Who else are you angry with? [*open question to probe*]
>
> PAT: Apart from you? John, Aneena – anyone who crosses my path.
>
> BRIAN: We are the people you express your anger to. But who are you really angry with? [*open question to challenge and hold frame of reference*]
>
> PAT: You . . . No . . . It's Peter. He shouldn't have left me – not like this.
>
> BRIAN: You're raging against Peter. [*paraphrase to affirm*]
>
> PAT: [*forcefully*] Yes! [*quietly*] And it's not fair. He didn't want to die.
>
> BRIAN: Peter has hurt you. He didn't want to die. But he has hurt you and you are angry with him. [*short summary*]

PAT: Yes . . . I guess that's it. I just hurt so much. It's a great aching void.

BRIAN: This is a terrible time for you to go through because you're facing your grief and all the misery and confusion it brings. I imagine that you do feel overwhelmed and confused at times.

PAT: Work is OK; it's the night that is worst when I am back home in the flat. I don't know whether I should start to clear away his things or just keep going as though he will return. Both seem impossible.

As the session proceeds, Brian gives Pat some information about transitions. She sees herself at a stage of acceptance where, although her feelings are intense, she is at a point of beginning to look ahead. Brian encourages Pat to use the energy that anger gives her to make what changes she feels able to. She decides that she needs to make contact with her longstanding friends, even if this means returning to the town where she and John lived together. On the practical level, she decides to leave things unchanged in the flat and, following a suggestion from Brian, to sit in Peter's usual chair. At least she won't be looking at the empty space left by Peter. Brian notes that he does not have to give much attention to transferring new insights and understanding into goals and action with Pat. This is something she appears well able to do herself. In contrast, this might be a major part of the work with other clients in similar situations, especially those whose grief has turned into depression.

Sessions 5 to 9

Brian notices a change in Pat. She still experiences waves of grief and anger but she is slowly becoming more outward looking. Pat describes her relationship with Aneena as 'up and down' but deepening. They are not only colleagues but also becoming good friends. Pat has also renewed contact with some of her old friends. She still finds contact with John, her former husband, very painful, and it stimulates uncontrollable levels of anger. She has decided to avoid him, until she feels more in control of her feelings. She is learning to use anger constructively as a way of lifting herself when she feels hopeless and helpless. After Session 9, Pat decides to see Brian less frequently and to phase the counselling down. She takes the option of seeing Brian when she is feeling particularly troubled.

Client's Reflections on Being Counselled

One year later, Pat still recalled the fourth session as being one of the most helpful. It marked the start of her regaining a less troubled sense of herself. Brian's responses to her anger and her irritation with him had helped Pat to accept that anger and grief often go together. Initially, Pat found it a comfort to be able to talk to somebody who understood how awful grieving can be. As the counselling progressed, she felt her experiences and feelings were accepted as valid. Brian wanted to understand her experiences from her own point of view and to help her with situations as she encountered them. She remembered this stage as one when she felt very supported and affirmed. As time went on, Pat realised that holding on to the possibility of talking to Brian was often a sufficient comfort in itself. Being counselled had reminded her of the value of being listened to, which was something she had little experience of in her adult life. Even Peter, who had given her a lot of encouragement, had treated her as though she were very similar to him rather than as a person in her own right. She still loved him and missed him but could now see some of the limitations of their friendship.

One of the consequences of counselling was that Pat came to appreciate how her bossiness sometimes prevented colleagues from talking about issues that concerned them. She began to adjust her communication style both at work and with friends so that she would listen more readily to their concerns. If the situation required firm leadership, she knew that she could still draw on her directness and assertiveness. Her relationship with colleagues improved as a result and some were becoming friends. For the time being, Pat decided that rebuilding her life following her separation from her husband and Peter's death was a greater priority than advancing her career. As she gradually rebuilt her life, she felt better able to take on new challenges at work. There were still times, such as Peter's birthday, when she felt desperately sad but these were becoming less frequent. Pat realised that it could be several years before she could think of either John or Peter without sorrow. She had started to sense an emerging self-respect and confidence in herself about the way that she was taking charge of her life.

Counsellor's Reflections on Using Counselling Skills in Formal Counselling

Brian developed a healthy respect for Pat and the way she coped with multiple losses. One of the challenges of working with her was deciding how to respond to her anger. He sometimes found her anger rather intimidating but was also aware of how it played a positive role in the way she coped. He discussed his reactions in supervision and acknowledged the differences between his and Pat's approach to their respective losses. Once again Brian was reminded that bereavement is such an intensely personal experience that what he had experienced might not be directly transferable to another person. As they got to know each other better, Brian was able to share his reactions with Pat. She responded in a typically robust and straightforward way. She had then wondered whether the combination of her grief-related anger and natural assertiveness was intimidating to others. Consequently, she reviewed the way in which she related to work colleagues and friends. Brian saw this as a major step in her rebuilding her life and establishing new contacts.

Brian had mixed feelings about seeing Pat less frequently. He found her both challenging and rewarding to work with and missed her. However, he was pleased that he had been able to play a role in helping Pat through her worst moments of grief and glad to see her progress and re-establish herself. He acknowledged that without Aneena's timely and sensitive intervention that opportunity might have been lost.

Manager's Reflections on Using Counselling Skills

Aneena was very glad to have had the skills to respond to Pat's enquiry about the sick note. She had no intimation that this enquiry would have such significance. Professionally, she was pleased to have retained a valuable member of staff on her team. She had also noticed that, as a consequence of her experiences, Pat had become much more sensitive in her working relationships with colleagues. She seemed more willing to listen and, as a result, there were fewer grumbles about her bossiness. Her capacity for leadership in moments of crisis had been gaining genuine respect. Pat was one of her team that Aneena trusted with complex work and viewed as a strong candidate for promotion. On a more personal level, she had appreciated having someone to talk to who was also coping with the death of a friend. She thought that their friendship was deep-rooted and would be long lasting.

There were moments when Aneena wanted to turn to Brian, as the staff counsellor, for advice. One such moment was when Pat and she were in such conflict about whether Pat should attend Peter's funeral. She had phoned Brian. He had been unwilling to discuss Pat directly because of confidentiality. However, he had been willing to discuss the process of bereavement in general terms and had explained how anger and sadness may be closely related. He also said that the way people cope with loss varies enormously between individuals and cultures. This discussion had helped Aneena to avoid taking Pat's anger as personal attacks and to distinguish between why attending funerals mattered so much to her but seemed much less important to Pat.

Conclusion

This case study provides glimpses into how counselling skills can be used to help someone through a significant bereavement. In this example, counselling skills enhanced the effectiveness of the line manager in responding appropriately to a team member.

The practitioner, working in a formal counselling setting, used the framework, together with his knowledge of the bereavement process, to inform his use of counselling skills.

In the next chapter, we will set out some additional information about a range of personally demanding situations, including bereavement, that can be helped by the sensitive and competent use of counselling skills.

8

DEMANDING SITUATIONS

Used adroitly, counselling skills can be immensely enabling to clients by offering them opportunities to explore issues that are causing concern and to find ways to a better future. They present the practitioner with powerful tools for engaging with complex issues and as such these skills can be both personally and professionally satisfying to acquire and use. However, the potency of these skills can expose us all to areas of human pain and difficulties for which we feel ill equipped, either by previous life experiences or existing expertise. It often feels like, and sometimes is, taking a 'step into the unknown'. This is in itself a personally demanding situation.

The situations raised by clients can be demanding in other ways. Often they will be raising issues for which they have been unable to find adequate support and help from their own social network. This may indicate that they are the types of issues for which help is not easily available in contemporary society. This may mean that practitioners have no readily accessible resources or knowledge on which to base their use of counselling skills. Our aim in writing this chapter is to provide some additional basic information that will be of immediate assistance as you step into the unknown to meet your client in his or her own experience. We have indicated some additional resources that we have found helpful in our work.

Feeling Overwhelmed and out of Control

We live in a culture that is favourably disposed to success, stamina and enthusiasm. It can be risky to talk about personal failure, difficulty or misery. In some settings and cultures, talking about personal difficulties involves such a loss of face and personal status that the deterrents to doing so are almost insurmountable. However personal distress is not easily contained and people do take the risk of disclosing deeply personal and painful matters, almost regardless of the consequences when they are sufficiently overwhelmed. All defences may be swept aside if the forces building up against them are sufficiently powerful. One of the risks of using counselling skills is that you may unleash a torrent of personal pain, with the consequence that you mirror the client's distress and begin to feel overwhelmed and out of control.

Over the years, we have observed a number of inappropriate responses to this kind of situation, responses that can compound the difficulties experienced by the client. For example:

- panicking and acting in ways that increase the sense of chaos or emergency for the client
- rushing to involve others regardless of the client's wishes or confidentiality
- collapsing into a personal sense of inadequacy and thus compounding the client's hopelessness
- ignoring the client's distress and searching for the positive or optimistic.

All these responses are unhelpful as well as potentially damaging to the client. In these instances it might help you to remember that:

- Listening is the finest compliment you can pay. Listening 'actively' is enabling because it allows others to have an impact on you at a time when they are feeling powerless; it acknowledges *them* as well as their experiences; and it affords them respect. Most importantly, it allows them to listen to themselves saying things that might be impossible to voice elsewhere.
- The client has identified you as someone who may be able to help them and, therefore, has recognised some personal quality or skill that they believe you possess. If this is not readily apparent, you might consider a well-timed question and ask why they have selected you or what they want from talking with you.
- The feelings elicited in you will be only a pale reflection of what the client is experiencing. Recognising the feelings elicited in you as a potentially valuable source of information about how the client is feeling can help you to gain the distance and 'objectivity' essential for effective helping. It will also be easier to suspend your own discomfort if you are adequately supported and know that you will be able to

attend to your own unresolved feelings and issues with a trusted colleague, a mentor or non-managerial supervisor.

Familiarity with counselling theory and practice will greatly help to give you confidence. One of the functions of this model is to bring a sense of order and containment to what are often initially frightening, complex and painful situations.

As you turn your attention to your client's feelings it may be helpful to know that there a number of things you can do that will be helpful to your client relatively early in your work together. Irvin Yalom (1995) identified eleven factors that help clients receiving psychotherapy. Three of these 'curative factors' are particularly relevant to the early stages of work with an acutely troubled client. These are:

1   the *instillation of hope*, which means communicating a sense of positive purpose to your encounter; a belief that change is possible; and that your client can act to improve or resolve any problems.
2   establishing a sense of *universality* to counter any sense of the client being uniquely alone with the problem or personally inadequate in having been unable to resolve it. You can do this by providing information or evidence that other people also experience the problem and how some have taken on the challenge of improving their situation.
3   providing opportunities for *catharsis* by the release or expression of feelings and reflecting on the experience of those feelings.

▶ Tips on how to cope with demanding situations

Sit in a centred position (become aware of your chair supporting you and feel the ground under your feet).

Raise your voice slightly; this will boost your energy and confidence.

Breathe slowly and calmly to reduce your anxiety.

Paraphrase, paraphrase and paraphrase! Empathy soothes tension.

Have some simple prompters ready; for example, 'Tell me more about . . .' 'Say some more . . .'

Acknowledge the 'rationale' of what the client is telling you so that you focus on understanding his or her experience.

Remind yourself that clients are responsible for their actions and their lives – not you.

Coping with Life Changes

Life is a continual sequence of changes, many of which are minor or incremental and may pass virtually unnoticed. Others, however, may be tougher because of their scale or significance. Typical of the latter are the 'life stage' changes, for example, negotiating adolescence; developing relationships such as forming a close attachment; coping with children leaving home to lead independent lives. Other significant changes might be in social or economic status often related to health or occupation; or involving a change of community or location, perhaps due to moving employment or home. There is growing body of research about the impact of change and the ways these can be negotiated successfully (Sugarman, 2001).

Experience and study suggests that:

- People respond very differently to seemingly similar levels of change in their lives. As a consequence, they experience differing levels of difficulty, often for no immediately apparent reasons. Listening to each person's unique experience is fundamental to helping them through.
- The same person may respond very differently to similar levels of change at different times in their lives.
- Unexpected changes or the simultaneous occurrence of several major changes complicates the process of integrating change.
- Positive changes can be as problematic as negative ones. This is so counter-intuitive that some feel particularly disorientated, sometimes to the point of doubting their sanity, when they experience emotional difficulties in handling positive changes such as winning a large prize, falling in love, the birth of a long awaited child, or a promotion.
- Being supported in a respectful and informed way through problematic transitions is beneficial and speeds up the transition process.

One model representing the transition process that has stood the test of time and, in our experience, provides useful background information for both practitioners and clients was developed by Hopson (1981). We have adapted this model and what follows is a description of the stages.

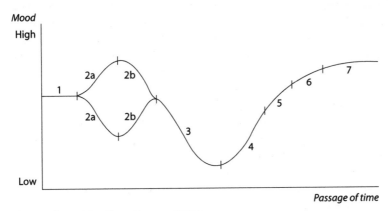

Phases of transition (from Hopson, 1981)

It is probably more accurate and helpful to regard each of the moments identified on the diagram as phases rather than strictly ordered and sequential points. The 'lived experience' of change and transition is often messier and more confused than the diagram suggests. Phases may blur into each other, run concurrently for a while or reappear periodically within a general progression through the process. The phases typically involve:

1 *Disbelief.* A time when the change seems unreal and unbelievable so that the emotional and cognitive responses are muted. The dominant experience is one of shock.

2 *Emotional reaction.* Feelings surge and there is a period of elation or despair (Point 2a) followed by these strong feelings being countered by their opposite (Point 2b). For example, delight at success might be dampened by doubts about being able to cope; sadness at failure might be tempered by relief at being under less pressure to succeed. At times clients may act as though the change has not occurred.

3 *Self-doubt.* During this phase the reality of what is happening begins to penetrate but the person concerned may be questioning how or whether they can respond. This phase is often associated with periods of anxiety, anger and apathy, sometimes with mood changes of disorientating rapidity. People may experience themselves as depressed. You will need your reflective skills and your exploration strategies to help someone through these first three stages.

4 *Emerging sense of new reality*. During this phase there is a movement from the focus on the past, evident in the earlier phases, to letting go in order to focus on the present. Sadness and anger may be experienced where the 'letting go' involves a sense of loss or injustice over the changes taking place. Strategies for reframing and introducing different perspectives become particularly relevant at this phase.

5 *Exploring the new situation*. The previous phase marks a first step towards accepting the new situation. This phase is concerned with exploring and testing new possibilities; the focus of the work centres on goals and constructing action plans.

6 *Searching for meaning*. Making sense of the changes and their causes is an important part of coming to terms with any major transition. It can be a time of learning and consolidating.

7 *Integration*. This is the point of acceptance and a sense of ease with the new situation. It marks the end of the transition.

Bereavement

Bereavement is perhaps the most emotionally troubling and painful transition to be negotiated. The very use of the term 'bereavement' is one way of marking the significance of the loss and the difficulty in what someone may be facing. The case study in Chapter 7 conveys both some of the pain that may be experienced and how using counselling skills can help those of us living in societies where there are few or no traditions to support mourning. Worden's classic text (2003) on grief counselling suggests four tasks that need to be accomplished during the grieving process. These tasks complement the process of responding to transitions.

The tasks are:

1 to accept the reality of the loss
2 to work through to the pain and the grief
3 to adjust to an environment in which the deceased is missing
4 to emotionally relocate the deceased and move on with life.

Worden's ideas and observations fit well with the values embodied in using counselling skills but his style of writing is one of the detached observer. In our experience, grieving is an intensely personal experience and this dimension is communicated better in Syme and Lendrum (1992) who draw on their own direct experience as well as on their work with clients.

The grieving process can be complicated by survivors having ambivalent feelings about the deceased persons; or by multiple bereavements occurring either simultaneously or in quick succession. Sudden or unexpected deaths create particular difficulties in the acceptance of the reality of the loss.

Bereavement by suicide is perhaps one of the most traumatic because of the legacy of guilt arising from 'if only . . . had done more' and the implied hostility or indifference of the deceased's feelings towards the survivors. Children also have very specific needs and ways of responding to bereavement (Worden, 2001). For one of the most helpful sources of up-to-date information on bereavement see http://www.crusebereavementcare.org.uk/publications.htm

Depression

Depression varies considerably in intensity. At its most severe, it may lead to someone lying inert in the foetal position for days, completely indifferent to whether they live or die or, perhaps more typically, to someone experiencing a combination of high levels of anguish and anxiety in conjunction with extreme lethargy. Severe depression of this kind requires assessment by a mental health professional, usually accessed through the General Practitioner or other health worker.

Counselling skills and strategies are appropriate to helping anyone experiencing depression who can talk about what they are experiencing, but they are particularly helpful with those whose depression is linked to their recent life events. Depression is a characteristic emotional state of the third phase of Hopson's transition model (see earlier in this chapter) and frequently occurs in bereavement. It may also be the result of being overwhelmed by an accumulation of personal or practical problems.

One of the characteristics of depression is a profound sense of helplessness. This has direct implications for using this counselling skills model. Depressed people often feel inundated and confused by their problems. Even when their difficulties are broken down into more manageable components, they may require assistance in deciding which aspect of the problem to tackle first. This is precisely the kind of situation for which focusing is an appropriate strategy (see Chapter 4).

However, focusing may need to be adapted to assist clients to overcome their sense of helplessness, especially if that helplessness has been learned in response to long-lasting problems. Instead of prioritising the issues to be addressed by their significance or urgency, it is usually more helpful to consider achievability and practical ease. Devise an agenda that moves from small first steps to progressively more demanding ones, and actively seek opportunities to support your clients' growing sense of achievement and self-confidence as they work through the agreed sequence. For example, a client feeling overwhelmed with a combination of debt and relationship problems might start by arranging an appointment with a debt counsellor, rehearsing how they are going to present the financial problems, attending the interview, and considering the outcome. The next step might be to start taking the first and easiest step to resolving the debt. Only when several steps have been taken towards addressing the more manageable problem would you consider addressing a more challenging issue, in this case the difficult relationship, in similarly progressive steps. The exact ordering of what seems manageable will depend on the client's perceptions, resources and previous experience.

Many of the standard texts that focus on helping people with depression tend to be written rather impersonally within the medical style of writing. A refreshingly accessible account, and one that is useful in helping people with depression, has been written by Rowe (2003), who views depression as a way of someone protecting themselves from pain and fear.

Suicidal Feelings

Anyone placed under sufficient pressure and deprived of adequate support has their breaking point and may contemplate suicide. Feeling suicidal is usually a time-limited phase that passes if the underlying problems can be adequately addressed. Counselling skills can be particularly appropriate for both providing the essential support and exploring a number of issues that may be helpful to the person concerned. The first barrier to be overcome is the cultural taboo on talking about suicidal intent. It is as though there is a belief that talking about this will increase the likelihood of someone implementing their self-destructive tendencies. The opposite is more likely to be the case. Someone who is unable to find appropriate support or to voice their sense of desperation is much more vulnerable to suicide.

One of the major tasks in helping someone who is feeling suicidal is to start to understand what the prospect of suicide represents. It may be an escape route to oblivion from an intolerable situation, in which case the priority is exploring whether and how the intolerable can be made more tolerable. It is common to find that suicidal intent is seldom as simple as that. The act of suicide may be envisaged as a means of communicating something that matters deeply to the client. For example, we have heard clients say, 'That will show them. They will be sorry that . . .' Where the suicidal intent is an indirect way of making a protest or expressing anger, exploring alternative and more effective ways of expressing these feelings and addressing the causes of them is an option.

One of the ways to empower someone who is feeling suicidal is to help him or her to identify the pressures that are making suicide a possible option. Typically the problems will have reached the point where they are overwhelming and form an insuperable barrier to any sense of hope for the future. Breaking larger problems down into parts and using the progressive problem-solving strategies suggested in response to depression may be of great assistance. Similarly it may be helpful to assist someone to prioritise which problem out of several problems is to be tackled first.

It is not unusual to find that there is not a deliberate and considered intent to die, but rather that life seems so intolerable that there is a willingness to gamble with death. With some people, it helps to regard suicidal intent as a signal that they cannot continue life as they are living it, and that a new start is required with some significant changes. You might want to explore, 'If your old life is dead, how do you want to live from now on? . . . What needs to change to make life more rewarding?' This will often generate a list of desired changes that can then be prioritised so that the person progressively works from what is most achievable to the bigger issues. A great deal of useful information and practical guidance can be found in a book based on the experience of Eldrid (1998) as the Director of the Samaritans in London, an international befriending service.

There seems to be no way of sharing in the suicidal person's burdens without leaving the helper weighed down and typically with a heightened sense of responsibility. Access to adequate support from someone experienced in working with suicidal people is essential for anyone undertaking this type of work.

Addictions

Addiction takes many forms. It may be addiction to nicotine, alcohol, or other legal and illegal substances. It may be an addiction to a particular behaviour such as work, gambling or pornography. The potential types of addiction appear endless. However there do seem to be a number of common principles to working with any type of addiction with people:

- Help is most effective where there is a sufficiently trusting relationship established with the helper. The helper may be someone who is further on in the process of managing their own addiction or someone who is more independent of the addiction. What matters is the level of trust.
- The addicted person needs to have reached a point where they can acknowledge both that they are 'out of control' and that it is having adverse effects on important aspects of his or her life. It is impossible to help someone who is denying that they have a problem. An acknowledgement that there is a problem to be faced, even if the intent to overcome it is ambivalent, is a much better starting point.
- Although no particular approach to working with addictions appears to be more successful than any other (Project Match Research Group, 1998), some general strategies are widely acknowledged as helpful. These approaches can be enhanced by using counselling skills and include:
  - providing information in ways tailored to clients' specific situations to maximise relevance. This is especially appropriate to the middle stage of the work.
  - working to resolve underlying issues that may have contributed to the addiction starting or being sustained
  - identifying strategies to reduce or eliminate the addictive behaviours including reduction of withdrawal symptoms or substituting alternative less self-damaging activities. Many different approaches use some form of structure based on the twelve-step approach used by Alcoholics Anonymous.
  - providing support to significant others such as family members or close friends who will benefit from a reduction in addictive behaviour. They have the double benefits of helping someone who matters in their lives to overcome addiction as well as an improvement in the quality of their relationship with the addicted person. Most agencies would only contact significant others with the client's support and consent.

Finding Further Information on Demanding Issues

Responding to the potential range of problems for which people seek help is a daunting challenge for any helper. Fortunately, the Internet has made obtaining information considerably easier. For example, if you go to www.google.co.uk (or any other search engine of your choice) and enter 'bullying' or 'domestic violence' you will have rapid access to a range of good and highly informative Web pages. The same is true of many other topics. The quality of the information available on the Web is very variable. It is not always easy to distinguish between good and poor information if you have no previous knowledge or experience of a subject. In this situation, it is often best to restrict yourself to information that has been provided by a reputable charity or agency, rather than sources that appear to be merely personal opinion. Having access to other people more experienced in helping with the specific issue raised by your client is invaluable in making sense of any source of information. Easy access to quality information can be of enormous assistance at any point in the process. However, during the Middle and Ending Stages of this model, as an aid both to reassessment and action planning, it is invaluable.

In some cases your clients may already be very knowledgeable about the issue that concerns them. However, using counselling skills is more than just being well informed. It is about developing the skills that will help you to facilitate someone through a process leading towards a constructive outcome.

9

ON BEING SUCCESSFUL IN USING COUNSELLING SKILLS

We have over 50 years' experience between us of using counselling skills and strategies in a great variety of settings and for different purposes. Our experience suggests that this model and the constituent strategies and skills are an invaluable addition to any helping or caring role. It is highly relevant and useful in circumstances:

• where you want to elicit clients' views and experiences rather than merely direct them towards a course of action
• where you consider a measure of joint problem-solving is appropriate
• when you believe that answers to resolving the problem lie primarily within the client.

The specific issues and problems to which the model can be applied successfully are enormously varied.

One question worth considering briefly is: having such a wide range of applications complicate identifying what constitutes success in using counselling skills? Surprisingly, there appear to be some common features across all successful applications. Characteristically, successful practitioners are both technically and relationally competent but, perhaps most importantly, are constantly open to and striving for new learning from both their experiences of using the skills and strategies as well as from their clients.

If you are learning counselling skills for the first time, you will maximise your learning opportunities by following the theory, strategies and skills suggested in this book. Some of the techniques may initially seem artificial and strange but as you become more confident in their impact you will be better placed to evaluate their relevance to your role and to adapt them to your preferred style. In our experience, the pace and focus of learning changes as you become more experienced. Your experience of the learning process will be modified as your proficiency and confidence grows. It will become more familiar and any negative feelings evoked by learning will become more fleeting.

Being 'Good Enough'

The optimum standard to be achieved in acquiring and using these skills is one of 'good enough'. An obsessive desire to seek perfection or to conform exactly to the model and guidance we have provided would be to miss the point of this book; and destine you and your clients to disappointment. Techniques cannot be understood or implemented independently of the relationship you construct with your clients and no two of these relationships will be the same. Maximising the help offered by using counselling skills requires simultaneous attention to both the intervention and the relationship. Over-emphasising technique will focus attention on the act of communicating and may obscure a sense of the client as a 'person' and the relationship you are forming. Over-sensitivity to the quality of the relationship may mean that the purposeful nature of the encounter is neglected, resulting in the use of inappropriate technique. The constant challenge of helping is being attentive to both technique and relationship. Both need to be balanced and held in the forefront of the practitioner's awareness. Sometimes these two aspects will seem to be in harmony and at other times in creative tension. This represents both the artistry and the discipline of using counselling skills.

The 'good enough' practitioner is sufficiently competent to be able to:

- take account of the existing quality of the relationship and work towards enhancing it
- identify the phase or stage reached in the helping relationship
- understand the strategies and skills appropriate to the particular stage of the helping relationship; selecting creatively from these strategies and skills and using them in ways that are compatible with the practitioner as a person
- use the strategies and skills productively and appreciate when they are having unexpected or unwanted effects
- constantly adapt and respond to the communications from the other person

- recover the helping process from mistakes either in using the skills or in developing the relationship
- evaluate strengths and weaknesses in the use of these skills with any particular client and support their evaluation with reasons.

The minimum aim of any training experience whether it is self-directed from literature and tapes or being supported by face-to-face tuition should be to take the participant to a basic level of competence. Attaining this basic level is both the first step in the learning process and also the point from which the practitioner becomes well placed to acquire further experience. During the early stages of acquiring unfamiliar counselling skills, implementing them will probably seem and feel awkward. Typical concerns include, 'Am I doing this right?' and 'Am I doing this at the right time?' or '. . . in the right circumstances?' The beginner's focus is, not unsurprisingly, on making the necessary progress towards becoming an effective 'doer'. The experience of learning is described in Chapter 1 in terms of progression through the four phases from 'unconscious incompetence' to 'unconscious competence'. At this latter stage the focus is on the learner's internal process.

Attaining a level of proficiency releases energy and allows the practitioner to contemplate a wider appreciation of the context in which the techniques and skills are deployed. It is at this juncture that the learning process changes in significant ways and is most suitably represented as a cycle of:

1 *Doing:* a technique is usually appropriately timed and adequately implemented at a good enough level of competence.
2 *Experiencing:* the practitioner observes the response that is evoked using both cognitive and emotional sources of information. This type of experiencing is sometimes referred to as a 'felt-sense'(Gendlin, 2003) that draws upon all the available sources of information. It is characteristic of experiential learning about working in relationship with clients that it involves both the learner's thoughts and feelings.
3 *Evaluating:* carefully considering, 'What went well?' 'What was unexpected?' 'What went badly?' and seeking the explanations for each evaluation.
4 *Refining:* specific instances of 'doing' are reinforced or adjusted in accordance with the evaluation. And so the cycle is renewed with the next instance of using the revised practice, until this too becomes unproblematic. At some point, only periodic appraisal may be required at less frequent intervals in order to avoid complacency.

The successful practitioner will continue to engage with this learning cycle so that the practice of counselling skills becomes a stimulus for further learning. Gradually the use of these skills becomes integrated into the 'person' of the practitioner, maturing and changing as the practitioner develops both personally and professionally.

One of the rewards of learning about and using counselling skills in this way is that there is no finite body of knowledge and skills to acquire that, once mastered, will gradually transform from being familiar to becoming stale and boring. Developing proficiency in counselling skills has the potential for continuing personal fulfilment and interest.

What Matters to Clients?

It is important not to become too precious about the nuances and subtleties of these strategies and skills. They may be an absorbing source of interest for the practitioner but it is worth remembering that when used well they become invisible to the client. Like a good musician, all the hard technical work that precedes a performance is transformed into something that appears effortless and flowing to an audience.

From the clients' perspective, what seems to matter is often much more fundamental and basic. It is clients' sense and experience of:

• you as a person and your personal qualities, including whether they experience you as sufficiently trustworthy to be the recipient of what they want to disclose
• your ability to relate to them, especially the quality of your listening and the attention that you give both to them and to what they tell you
• the level of safety that you provide that allows them to be vulnerable and to experiment with new possibilities. Clients are often looking for the personal equivalent of a safe harbour in a storm or an anchor in a running sea.

Don't take our word for this. Ask your clients. You may be as surprised as we have been by their answers. You may be astounded by the examples of wisdom and knowledge that are offered to you by your clients, as well as surprised at some of the misunderstandings that might have otherwise gone unmentioned.

Clients' views are important. It is the work with our clients that justifies the investment of time and resources in acquiring and using counselling skills. The views of our clients are probably the best possible foundation on which to build our development as practitioners and users of counselling skills.

References

Aldridge, S., Rigby, S. and Tribe, L. (eds) (2001) *Counselling Skills in Context.* London: Hodder and Stoughton.

Argyle, M. (1988) *Bodily Communication.* London: Routledge.

Bond, T. (1989) 'Towards defining the role of counselling skills', *Counselling: Journal of the British Association for Counselling,* 69: 24–6.

Bond, T. (2000) *Standards and Ethics for Counselling in Action.* London: Sage.

Culley, S. (1991) *Integrative Counselling Skills in Action.* London: Sage.

Daines, B., Gask, L. and Usherwood, T. (1997) *Medical and Psychiatric Issues for Counsellors.* London: Sage.

d'Ardenne, P. and Mahtani, A. M. (1999) *Transcultural Counselling in Action,* 2nd edn. London: Sage.

Dryden, W. (1989) *Key Issues for Counselling in Action.* London: Sage.

Dryden, W. (1999) *Rational Emotive Behavioural Counselling in Action,* 2nd edn. London: Sage.

Dryden, W. and Feltham, C. (1992) *Brief Counselling: A Practical Guide for Beginning Practitioners.* Buckingham: Open University Press.

Egan, G. (2002) *The Skilled Helper: A Problem-Management and Opportunity-Development Approach to Helping,* 7th edn. New York: Wadsworth.

Eldrid, D. (1998) *Caring for the Suicidal.* London: Constable.

Elton-Wilson, J. (1996) *Time-Conscious Counselling and Psychotherapy.* Chichester: Wiley.

Freshwater, D. (2003) *Counselling Skills for Nurses, Midwives and Health Visitors.* Milton Keynes: Open University Press.

Gendlin, E.T. (1996) *Focusing-Oriented Psychotherapy.* New York: Guilford Press.

Gendlin, E.T. (2003) *Focusing: How to Open up Your Deeper Feelings and Intuition.* London: Vintage/Ebury.

Gilmore, S.K. (1973) *The Counselor-in-Training.* Englewood Cliffs, NJ: Prentice-Hall.

Hawkins, P. and Shohet, R. (2000) *Supervision in the Helping Professions,* 2nd edn. Milton Keynes: Open University Press.

Hopson, B. (1981) 'Response to the papers by Schlossberg, Brammer and Abrego', *Counselling Psychologist,* 9: 36–9.

Hopson, B. and Scally, M. (1982) *Life Skills Teaching Programmes,* No. 2. Leeds: Life Skills Associates.

Jacobs, M. (1998) *Presenting Past,* 2nd edn. Milton Keynes: Open University Press.

Jenkins, P. (1997) *Counselling, Psychotherapy and the Law*. London: Sage.

King, G. (1999) *Counselling Skills for Teachers*. Milton Keynes: Open University Press.

Lago, C. and Smith, B. (2003) *Anti-discriminatory Counselling Practice*. London: Sage.

Lago, C. and Thompson, J. (1996) *Race, Culture and Counselling*. Buckingham: Open University Press.

Lewin, K. (1969) 'Quasi-stationary social equilibria and the problem of permanent change', in W.G. Bennis, K.D. Benne and R. Chin (eds), *The Planning of Change*. New York: Holt, Rinehart and Winston.

Lister Ford, C. (2002) *Skills in Transactional Analysis Counselling and Psychotherapy*. London: Sage.

McLeod, J. (2003) *An Introduction to Counselling*, 3rd edn. Buckingham: Open University Press.

Mearns, D. and Dryden, W. (eds) (1990) *Experiences of Counselling in Action*. London: Sage.

Mearns, D. and Thorne, B. (1999) *Person-Centred Counselling in Action*, 2nd edn. London: Sage.

Mearns, D. and Thorne, B. (2000) *Person-Centred Therapy Today: New Frontiers in Theory and Practice*. London: Sage.

Mickelson, D. and Stevic, R. (1971) 'Differential effects of facilitative and non facilitative behavioural counsels', *Journal of Counseling Psychology*, 18: 314–19.

Munro, A., Mantei, B. and Small, J. (1989) *Counselling: The Skills of Problem-Solving*. London: Routledge.

Nelson-Jones, R. (1996) *Effective Thinking Skills*. London: Sage.

Nelson-Jones, R. (2000) *Introduction to Counselling Skills*. London: Sage.

Nelson-Jones, R. (2002) *Essential Counselling and Therapy Skills*. London: Sage.

Oldfield, S. (1983) *The Counselling Relationship: A Study of the Client's Experience*. London: Routledge and Kegan Paul.

Palmer, S. and McMahon, G. (eds) (1997) *Client Assessment*. London: Sage.

Pedersen, P.B., Draguns, J.G., Lonner, W.J. and Trimble, J.E. (eds) (1996) *Counseling Across Cultures*, 5th edn. Thousand Oaks, CA: Sage.

Ponterotto, J.G., Casas, J.M., Suzuki, L.A. and Alexander, C.M. (eds) (1995) *Handbook of Multicultural Counselling*. London: Sage.

Project Match Research Group (1998) 'Matching alcoholism treatments to client heterogeneity: Project MATCH three year drinking outcomes', *Alcoholism: Clinical and Experimental Research*, 22: 1300–1311.

Reddy, M. (1987) *The Manager's Guide to Counselling at Work*. London: Methuen.

Rogers, C.R. (1951) *Client-Centered Therapy: Its Current Practice, Implications and Theory*. London: Constable.

Rogers, C.R. (1961) *On Becoming a Person*. Boston: Houghton Mifflin.

Rogers, C.R. (1980) *A Way of Being*. Boston: Houghton Mifflin.

Ross, A. (2003) *Counselling Skills for Church and Faith Community Workers*. Milton Keynes: Open University Press.

Rowan, J. (1998) *The Reality Game*, 2nd edn. London: Routledge.

Rowe, D. (2003) *Depression: The Way Out of Your Prison*. Hove: Brunner-Routledge.

Steiner, C. (1997) *Achieving Emotional Literacy*. London: Bloomsbury.

Stewart, I. (2000) *Transactional Analysis Counselling in Action*. London: Sage.

Stewart, I. and Joines, V. (1987) *TA Today: A New Introduction to Transactional Analysis*. Nottingham: Lifespace.

Sugarman, L. (2001) *Life-Span Development: Frameworks, Accounts and Strategies*. Hove: Psychology Press.

Syme, G. and Lendrum, S. (1992) *Gift of Tears: A Practical Approach to Loss and Bereavement Counselling*. London: Routledge.

Tolan, J. (2003) *Skills in Person-Centred Counselling and Psychotherapy*. London: Sage.

Trower, P., Casey, A. and Dryden, W. (1988) *Cognitive Behavioural Counselling in Action*. London: Sage.

Truax, C.B. and Carkhuff, R.R. (1967) *Towards Effective Counselling and Psychotherapy Training and Practice*. Chicago: Aldine.

Tschudin, V. (1995) *Counselling Skills for Nurses*. London: Elsevier.

Watzlawick, P., Weakland, J.H. and Fisch, R. (1974) *Change: Principles of Problem Formation and Problem Resolution*. London: Norton.

Woof, W.R. and Carter, Y.H. (1997a) 'The grieving adult and the general practitioner: a literature review in two parts (Part 1)', *British Journal of General Practice*, 47: 443–8.

Woof, W.R. and Carter, Y.H. (1997b) 'The grieving adult and the general practitioner: a literature review in two parts (Part 2)', *British Journal of General Practice*, 47: 509–514.

Worden, J.W. (2001) *Children and Grief: When a Parent Dies*. New York: Guilford.

Worden, J.W. (2003) *Grief Counselling and Grief Therapy: A Handbook for the Mental Health Practitioner*, 3rd edn. London: Brunner-Routledge.

Yalom, I.D. (1995) *Theory and Practice of Group Psychotherapy*. New York: Basic Books.

Yalom, I.D. (2001) *The Gift of Therapy*. London: Piatkus.

Index